SINGLE HANDED

SINGLE HANDED

THE OBSERVER/EUROPE 1 SINGLEHANDED TRANSATLANTIC RACE

EDITED BY LIBBY PURVES AND TREVOR GROVE

INTRODUCTION BY ERIC TABARLY

EBURY PRESS LONDON

Published by Ebury Press
National Magazine House
72 Broadwick Street
London W1V 2BP

First impression 1984

ISBN 0 85223 430 9

A PHOEBE PHILLIPS EDITIONS BOOK

Filmset by Tradespools Limited
in Frome, Somerset

Colour separations by Preager Blackmore Limited
in Eastbourne, Sussex

Printed and bound in Belgium
by Offset-Printing van den Bossche N.V.

EDITORS' FOREWORD

This book is a tribute to the world's oldest singlehanded ocean sailing race from the world's oldest Sunday newspaper. The links between OSTAR and *The Observer* were forged even before the inaugural cannon was fired to mark the start of the first Observer Singlehanded Transatlantic Race back in 1960. There had been many months of plotting and planning between the man who first dreamed up the race, Blondie Hasler, and the then Editor of *The Observer*, David Astor, before a yacht club could be found to organize the contest. Once the Royal Western Yacht Club had boldly agreed to hold the event under its auspices, there was still a great deal to be thought about and done: rules had to be drawn up (though it was fundamental to Hasler's concept that there should be as few of these as possible); safety factors had to be considered; contenders needed to be found for a race which in those days sounded unprecedentedly dangerous and demanding.

As the sailing world knows, the 1960 OSTAR rapidly evolved into a four-yearly competition which now ranks as the premier event of its kind. What is more, it gave such a boost to the sport of shorthanded sailing, especially in France, that there has since grown up a whole international circuit of such races. The names of the top singlehanded skippers have become as famous as those of footballers and athletes. Advances in boat design inspired by the requirements of solo racing have had benefits for small craft sailors everywhere. Yachting as a whole, from Cowes Week to the America's Cup, has vastly increased in popular appeal thanks partly to the intense interest created by singlehanded racing, where sailing is pared down to its barest and toughest elements.

We decided at an early stage that this quarter-century celebration of OSTAR should not take the form of a straightforward history by a single author. We felt it would be of greater interest to allow the book to be shaped by the event itself, by those who had taken part in it or written about it at key moments in the saga.

In crucial respects, every race has been different from every other: rules have altered and evolved, new designs have been introduced, safety and navigational aids have become increasingly sophisticated; the French radio station Europe 1 joined *The Observer* as co-sponsors in 1980. And there has always been that unique and unpredictable factor, the weather. Each time the event has been held, therefore, it has had to be looked at with different eyes — eyes screwed up against North Atlantic storms or dazzled by new technological marvels, saddened by tragedy or alight with triumph.

So we turned first to those of whom it could be said: they were there, they saw it happen... We chose the best articles we could find from *The Observer*, from other British publications and from *Sail*, the Boston magazine that has taken a particular interest in OSTAR. We made few editorial adjustments to bring them up to date or alter the perceptions of the moment. We were anxious not to lose that vital quality of immediacy.

At the same time, we didn't want the book to be merely an anthology of past sailing yarns. The race that was about to start in June 1984, as this volume began to take shape, was certain to prove the most dramatic to date, if only because of the astonishing advances in equipment and design. We not only needed a report on it: we also wanted to use the 1984 OSTAR as a sort of literary telescope through which to view the progress of the race since its inception. So we wrote about the start and the preparations for it at Millbay Dock; and we were at Newport to wait for the finishers and to greet the winners. In Plymouth, we went aboard *Jester*, the only boat that has taken part in every race. We asked yachting writer and OSTAR participant Geoff Hales to consider the technical evolution of the race from 1960 to 1984 – and he did so into a tape-recorder while actually at sea, before he was forced to retire with (ironically) equipment failure. We also took a long look at sponsorship, a matter of stormy controversy from the first time a boat carried the name of a product on her bows.

The Observer Singlehanded Transatlantic Race has been much photographed, increasingly so as the event gained popularity and as the specially designed craft grew more outlandish. At the 1984 start there were no fewer than 16 helicopters dodging dangerously about just a few hundred feet above our heads. At Newport as the winners crossed the line the photographers were out in force again, dicing with 15-knot trimarans in tiny speedboats. The difficulty in selecting the pictures for this book, therefore, has been in choosing rather than in finding those photographs that best convey the spirit of the race.

It is nearly 25 years since OSTAR began. It has already won its place in the history of yachting and human daring. This book looks back at how that place was won.

We also hope it will provide a vantage point from which to look ahead – to the next quarter century in the history of this remarkable race.

TREVOR GROVE, LIBBY PURVES

LIBBY PURVES
is a writer, journalist and BBC broadcaster who has herself sailed the Atlantic.

CHRISTOPHER BRASHER
is a sports writer and ex-Sports Editor of *The Observer*.
A gold-medal-winning Olympic athlete, he was the originator of the London Marathon.

ALISTAIR COOKE
is best known to BBC listeners for his 'Letter from America'. He is also a distinguished
author and was for many years *The Guardian*'s chief US correspondent.

MURRAY SAYLE
is an author and journalist, and was formerly a senior feature writer
on *The Sunday Times*. He took part and was dismasted in the 1972 OSTAR.

MICHAEL DAVIE
is an *Observer* columnist. He was previously Editor of the *Melbourne Age* and
Deputy Editor of *The Observer*.

ALAIN COLAS
was the outstanding French sailor who won the 1972 OSTAR and came second in 1976
aboard the giant *Club Méditerranée*. He was lost at sea in 1978.

PHIL WELD
won the 1980 OSTAR at the age of 65 (the first American winner). He was a journalist
before becoming a newspaper publisher and passionate multihull enthusiast.

JUDY LAWSON
is an American yachting writer and former dinghy sailor, well known in
international racing circles.

FRANK PAGE
was *The Observer*'s yachting correspondent for several years, and has himself written
two books about OSTAR.

JIM BROWN
is a designer and occasional contributor to *Sail* magazine.

GEOFF HALES
is a sailing writer, broadcaster and journalist, as well as a veteran singlehander.
He was forced to retire from the 1984 race.

BOB FISHER
is presently yachting correspondent for *The Observer*, *The Guardian* and the BBC.

HUGH McILVANNEY
is one of *The Observer*'s best-known writers, who has on several occasions won the
top British newspaper awards for his sports reports and features.

TREVOR GROVE
is Editor of the *Observer Magazine*.

Art Director
CLIVE CROOK of *The Observer*
Assisted by Cherriwyn Magill

CONTENTS

High tech at high speed: the latest generation of big trimarans can do 25 knots or more. Before the 1984 race Jeff Houlgrave warned that the one thing these highly tuned racers were vulnerable to was damage at sea: 'Colt Cars G.B.' was dismasted and had to be abandoned

CARS G.B.
22

INTRODUCTION
Eric Tabarly

Before 1960 singlehanded crossings of the North Atlantic from west to east were relatively numerous. But I have heard of only a few in the opposite direction which did not follow a very southerly trade-winds route. Of the two best-chronicled the first was Alain Gerbault in 1923 aboard *Firecrest*. He took a fairly southerly course, his passage taking him through Bermudan waters. This course kept him in the region of the prevailing westerly winds, but it allowed him to take advantage of far more clement conditions than are to be found further north. The other famous single-hander was Royal Navy Commander R.D. Graham, who in 1934 journeyed from Ireland to Newfoundland in 24 days. This was a much shorter route than Plymouth to Newport, but right in the path of the depressions.

The scarcity of singlehanded attempts at this voyage underlined its difficulty. It was this fact which tempted Blondie Hasler when he had the idea of proposing a race from England to America.

Since then, other singlehanded races have been conceived but OSTAR, with its unique combination of challenging winds and depressions, remains the most testing, both for men and equipment. For this reason, in my view, it remains the finest race, even if some years are more merciful than others, and even if the Argos satellite system has changed the character of the race.

Clearly, no sailor now awaits the OSTAR start in quite the same state of anticipation as was once the case. Before, each skipper knew that in an emergency there would probably be no one to come to the rescue; now he or she only has to trigger off the distress signal and wait to be picked up. Personally, I regret this new element of safety, which relegates those vital qualities of an ocean-going yacht – namely strength and seaworthiness – to second place, in favour of pure speed. Happily, once again this year, in spite of very mild weather conditions, it was the most seamanlike boats that came in first. The true character of the race remains unscathed.

This race has been and remains the most exacting test of its kind – because of the course, and because of the number and quality of its competitors. It richly merits having its story told in this thoroughly researched and up-to-date account.

September 1984

By tradition, contestants in the Observer/Europe 1 Singlehanded Transatlantic Race spend their last few days before the start tied up at one of Plymouth's least glamorous quaysides. For the skippers they are days of prolonged tension, after which the starter's cannon will come as a relief. Libby Purves, who has herself sailed the Atlantic and reported on previous OSTAR starts for the BBC, was at Millbay Dock on the eve of the 1984 race.

AT MILLBAY DOCK
Libby Purves

Millbay Dock in Plymouth is not a glamorous location. The gas storage cylinders, the piled-up cubes of crushed motor-cars and the long, gritty and windswept approach from the city centre do not lend it any charm. For most of the time, any yacht laid up in the Inner Basin condemns itself to spend further days in cleaning layers of rusty scrapyard dust off every inch of its deck and rigging; outside the lock gate, on the club buoys, small boats plunge and roll uneasily in any stiff southerly blow from beyond the breakwater. Comfort-loving yachtsmen avoid the whole place and take their custom gratefully to one of the marinas.

But another four years have passed, and Millbay has come into its quadrennial OSTAR flowering. The tangles of exhausts and rusting chassis are hidden discreetly behind plastic sheeting and blue-and-white bunting; the brief, meretricious glitter of hot-dog vans, trade stalls, sponsor's cars and a striped press tent has transformed this dour piece of abandoned dockland into a street fair. For a week at the end of May, the holiday crowds ebb and flow around the stagnant basin, buying ice-creams and sodas, trying on bargain Guernseys, restraining excited children from falling into the dock, laughing and chattering and pointing at the boats.

For Millbay is cheerfully busy for once. The rules of The Observer/Europe 1 Singlehanded Transatlantic Race stipulate that yachts must arrive a week ahead of the start for inspection in Millbay; and the great majority stay there until towed out through the narrow entrance on the last high water before the gun. To each contestant there is some comfort in the proximity of 91 others bound to face the same ocean in the same solitude; for the milling public on the dock's edge, the fleet provides an incomparable spectacle: a boat show of bizarre variety, with a pleasing edge of high drama.

The race entries range from tiny boats looking

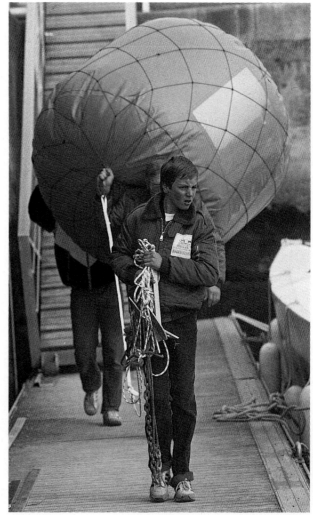

Preceding pages and above: Millbay Dock before the 1984 race

like sailing dinghies, clumsily finished off in home workshops, through cosy, affluent family cruisers with sprigged curtains and galley garlic presses to the last word in Formula I high-technology speed machines. It is as if you could put your old family pony in for the Derby, or try out an old Ford against a Lotus or Mercedes on the Grand Prix circuit.

*American contestant
Robert Scott aboard his 40ft
monohull 'Lands End'*

Peter Phillips: first Briton home in 1984

Mike Richey: he bought 'Jester' from Blondie Hasler

Eric Loizeau: his trimaran had to retire in 1984

Some of the less lovable members of the top international ocean-racing circuit would like to see the race remodelled to exclude the so-called 'no-hopers' at the amateur end of the fleet; but the Royal Western Yacht Club continues to stipulate only seaworthiness and a competent skipper.

Gratefully, the spirit of Blondie Hasler and Francis Chichester still holds; it is not so much that the skippers of these slow boats have no hopes, it is simply that their hopes are different. And when the week is over and they sail out of this rackety funfair into the rushing silence of the Atlantic, each one will be as much alone as the biggest international sailing star, hanging on to the same one life.

This latest year sees a clearer distinction of boats than ever before; the multihulls form 40 per cent of the fleet and almost fill Class I, the largest boats and the most likely outright winners. The smaller and slower the boat, the more it usually looks like the conventional idea of a yacht: single-hulled, solid,

June Clarke: her 'Batchelor's Sweet Pea' capsized

Tony Bullimore: 'City of Birmingham'

John Mansell: abandoned ship in the 1984 OSTAR

modestly rigged. In the dock, a central pontoon accommodates a mass of these, together with the smaller catamarans, huddled cheerfully together as they might be in any holiday marina. A crouching figure adjusts a steering-vane on *La Baleine* (Trinidad and Tobago); a crowd of children climbs proudly aboard *Tyfoon* (Belgium); friends shout from *La Peligrosa* (Holland) and *Moustache* (Canada); a skipper high up on his mast, adjusting the spreaders, shouts some greeting, whipped away

by the wind, towards a face and a wave on the dockside. Children row around in rubber dinghies, self-importantly pointing out hero daddies; trolleysful of tinned curry sauce and six-packs of beer are transferred down hatches with a blithe disregard for deadweight. José Ugarte from Spain climbs across two decks in order to leave a message in a neighbour's tiny cabin, and the American flag waves over cartons of Coke.

Around the edges of the dock it is quieter. The

Above: Belgian 1984 entry 'Tyfoon VI', skippered by 55-year-old boatbuilder Gustave Versluys
Below: Thomas Veyron's tiny 30ft trimaran 'Rizla +', one of the two smallest multihulls in the 1984 OSTAR

Above: British monohull 'Abacus', with Jerry Freeman at the helm
Below: 1984's smallest skipper, Monique Brand, with non-finisher 'Aliance Kaypro'

Jeff Houlgrave hangs from the mast that was to let him down at sea in 1984

great spidery floats of the trimarans keep them apart from each other, not tucked cosily cabin to cabin. Uniformed support teams swarm over the biggest machines; far up *Paul Ricard*'s mast a lonely figure struggles to tape up the third set of spreaders, the race-flag flapping awkwardly around his head. Her skipper, the legendary Eric Tabarly, twice the winner of this race, has not been spotted yet around the dock; his support team, in Ricard anoraks and moving invariably at the jog-trot, breeze all day in and out of the biggest hotel, and flash past in team cars. Of course, Geoff Hales, down from the mast of his tubby catamaran *Quest for Charity*, has a support team too. He is collecting for five charities, and seems surrounded all day by motherly ladies

with tins to rattle. A posse in pink is round him now, presenting a bottle of Scotch. 'Oh, thank you. Thank you. Yes, one does feel a bit silly doing it again, but it gets into the system. Must go, I have to do my end-of-year accounts for the business.' Doing up a stray shackle, he scrambles below to his accounts. An hour later, inevitably, the boat's capacious deck will once more be creaking with well-wishers and charity collectors.

Fifty yards away, in brooding concentration, teams of technicians work on the big racers: scrubbing the hull of *Colt Cars GB*, fitting wires below on *Crédit Agricole II*, swabbing down hydro-foil shapes, bending anxiously over hydraulic tensioners.

Eric Loizeau, whose high hopes for 'Roger & Gallet' were not realized

Marc Pajot, second man home in 1984, aboard his monster catamaran 'Elf Aquitaine II'

The undoubted showpiece of the year, the crowdpuller, what the technical writers hail as 'the quantum leap in boatbuilding', is *Elf Aquitaine II*, the catamaran sailed by France's highest paid sportsman, Marc Pajot. Above its 60ft twin floats and X-shaped crossbeam strung with net, knots of sightseers stand all day, chattering with more or less knowledge about its futuristic appearance. We gaze at the vast aerofoil mast, like a red-and-white aeroplane wing standing on end; at its rotating boom and infinitely variable sheeting; we cautiously discuss slots and tack positioning and the months of wind-tunnel testing behind the monster's shape. 'Not as heavy up there as it looks', says a man in baggy pink yachting trousers, gazing doubtfully

skywards, 'Carbon fibre, you see.' 'Well, I wouldn't go far in it', avers his wife, backing away. Below them, indifferently, booted and knived deckhands hose down the floats for the third time that day. My son, 18 months old, is wheeled round the dock for a quick appraisal. 'Boat', he intones, passing each mast. Except *Elf Aquitaine II*. After a pause, he reclassifies it firmly, 'Air-plane.' We peer cautiously into the cramped twin cabins; every piece of gear, every mug and plate and instrument, down to the

Overleaf: Two views of France's singlehanded hero Eric Tabarly with hydrofoiler 'Paul Ricard', his entry in the 1984 OSTAR. Tabarly has won the race twice – in 1964 and 1976

Nagrafax weather recorder, is exactly duplicated in each hull; Pajot need not live to leeward, ever. 'I suppose if he'd left his detective story there, half-finished, he might crawl across the net for it?' said the wife of the man in pink trousers, doubtfully. 'Or would he have two?'

Boats like *Elf* make the last generation of multihulls look oddly muted and quaint. Two years ago, *Colt Cars GB* was the latest thing; Rob and Naomi James scored a brilliant Round Britain win in her. Now Jeff Houlgrave is sailing her to Newport. 'You push. You push within an inch of damage to get success. Push yourself beyond a limit you didn't even know you'd got.'

His sleeping arrangements he describes as 'park bench minimal'; a bean-bag on wooden slats. *Colt Cars* might win for Britain, even against the 16 threatening Class I Frenchmen. 'I don't', says Houlgrave firmly to a television crew, 'actually like the French, particularly.'

The memory of Rob James (drowned in a fall from *Colt Cars*, freakishly, in the very entrance to Salcombe harbour after safely mastering oceans) suddenly brings back other visions of the ghosts of Millbay Dock; remembered faces from the past, weeks just like this in the wind and the sunshine, amid the crowds and the fluttering flags. Just where the new pontoon is now, Rob's little flyer *Boatfile* lay next to his wife's *Kriter Lady* in 1980, and they sat together laughing as Naomi announced to reporters that she had only entered the race herself to take her mind off worrying about Rob during it. Where *City of Birmingham* now spreads its three bright red hulls used to be Angus Primrose's berth in *Demon Demo* in 1976 and *Demon of Hamble* in 1980. Both were invariably loaded below their marks with chattering, celebrating British parties, surrounding the extrovert host; he too is lost now, not on the race but on another West Indian voyage. Nor will the yellow hulls of Mike McMullen's 1976 *Three Cheers* be seen here again; the only wreckage was found four years later, off Iceland.

The Observer Singlehanded has not been a race of many deaths; but the sea will claim its adversaries at any time. Another melancholy memory was of David Blagden: the smallest entry ever in the tiny *Willing Griffin*, he was also one of the bravest; he finished triumphantly in 52 days, but died in the Irish sea a couple of years later.

'Men admit fear, in a situation like this. Usually they don't admit it, but it seems all right when they're facing this', said Alan Wynne Thomas's young wife, who sailed across with him and both their children last year. 'I can see that he sweats, sometimes.' But Alan has wanted to do the race since 1960; this year his family cruiser *Jemima Nicholas* must fulfil that dream by becoming a Class

Britain's top hope for 1984, ex-policeman Peter Phillips aboard 'Travacrest Seaway'. He fell overboard, but managed to clamber back to safety

Above: Alan Perkes' 'Sherpa Bill'; the flowers and garden gnome add a homely touch to the cockpit
Below: Philippe Poupon, first across the line but later relegated to second place

Above: Patrick Morvan, whose 'Jet Services' led the 1984 fleet until disaster – a floating tree trunk – struck
Below: Chris Butler, who brought 'Swansea Bay' into Newport to take first place in Class V

ACHILLES 840

'Umupro Jardin' gets off to a flying start in June 1984. The big multis soon left spectator launches behind

III starter. Alan bounds up to his wife with his friend, Tim Hubbard from *Johan Lloyde*, in tow. Both wear T-shirts saying GO FOR BROKE WITH THE HALF CROWN CLUB. 'We are returning to the original Hasler bet', they announce. 'We are sick of total sponsorship and needle. Our club motto is' (another T-shirt appears) 'IT'S ONLY A SPRINT'.

They were at the Mayflower marina, where a handful of boats lay berthed some distance from the main dock, but they shuttled amiably to and from Millbay, at one with the main fleet in spirit if not in geography. David Ryan, on the other hand, a silent Rhode Islander, docked *Phagawi* there deliberately. After a miserable arrival – the shipping company actually freighted the wrong yacht to Le Havre to meet him, and he had to return and travel alongside his real boat, working on her all the way – Ryan tied up in splendid isolation in the Mayflower, repelling press and visitors alike. 'All that camaraderie's a waste of time.'

Farther down the pontoon, Paul Lindenberg, designer of Warren Luhrs's revolutionary water-ballasted monohull *Thursday's Child*, was happy to adjust the boom and show off the extraordinary pendulum rudder and water-ballast tanks controlled on each tack from the cockpit. 'I have sailed across with Warren in 17 days', says the designer.

'We make near 30 knots off the wind.' It must be frustrating to see one's design sail off without one, on such a challenge, I suggested. 'Ah no. I think I prefer to go by plane.'

Back at Millbay, the relaxed atmosphere of midweek has evaporated: it is Friday; out beyond Drake's Island the weather is beginning to threaten a hard blow at the start. Last-minute crises erupt. Florence Arthaud's *Biotherm II*, dismasted on the way over, is being repaired by eight boatbuilders flown in from France. Meanwhile, aboard the tiny *Jester*, Michael Richey has discovered that one of his 11 wine-boxes is not Côtes du Rhône at all, but rosé. A hasty test proves the rest are mercifully sound. On *Race Against Poverty*, Chris Smith has checked his advanced water-ballasting arrangements, talked to a dozen reporters about his efforts to raise £50,000 for Intermediate Technology, posed next to a sample dugout canoe designed for Third World fishermen, and is now negotiating a weekly call from the *Today* radio programme about his progress. 'Though you don't know', he says with Christian fortitude, 'whether they'll ever broadcast one single word of it.' He is a dentist, this his third race; a Methodist lay-preacher, invincibly cheerful. I tell him about my own careful arrangements back in 1980 to make Naomi James's conversations with the *Today* programme easy for her – how I stood by reserved telephones in a reserved studio for six hours a week, waiting for Portishead to make contact – and he shudders. 'People in offices don't really understand about this race, what it's like. They think it's a yachting event. Yachting is a rich man's sport, so it's comfortable, so you can wait your turn.' Still, Smith is very cheerful; tipped by both *The Observer* and *Yachting Monthly* commentators to win his class. 'I'm basking in that. Oh yes.'

All along the central pontoon, in the windy sunshine of this last day, the more sociable boats are still crowded, each party crumbling crisps and slopping cans of beer over what will tomorrow night be one human being's private universe. Will their giggling ghosts seem, when the skipper is tired and perhaps hallucinating after the long first night's anxiety of the Land's End shipping lanes, to be sitting there still?

News has gone up on the board that the largest number of icebergs on record is moving south from the Arctic to threaten the fast northern routes. The press is pleased to have this extra story; the skippers look decidedly glum. Someone is playing back a cassette of a radio broadcast to a gang of friends. 'This is June Clarke's boat', says the announcer jovially. 'Oh look, someone's just climbing out of

the bunk.' 'He's mending the radio', says Ms Clarke with severity. A burst of ribald laughter around the cassette machine. In the coffee bar, more ribaldry as a group of skippers and pressmen fill in specimen questionnaires handed out by some medical Italians, wishing to record food and drink taken each day, frequency of urine and bowel motions, colour of same, and other intimacies. Unrepeatable, joyful, lavatorial jokes erupt.

Walter Greene ('Kermit' to his entourage, builder of last time's winner, *Moxie*) explains his new catamaran's self-righting system to a group of technical writers; at the other side of the basin, his publicity agent is hunting for him with decreasing hope. *Biotherm*'s new mast is progressing more slowly than was hoped; in their promotional tent, Biotherm team girls with flawless complexions endlessly re-run a beautiful video of Florence Arthaud, silhouetted against her sails in the sunset, glamorous and free. The real Arthaud, unnoticed, drawn and shabby with three days of strained uncertainty when her mast and float were damaged on the way to Plymouth, runs past to a waiting car. An overwhelming smell of aniseed wafts downwind from the Ricard caravan; a new crowd has gathered, silently, around the big foiler, though not to examine its wave-cheating hydrofoils and spoilers

Setting course for Newport after the 1984 start: most of the monohulls were left bobbing in the multis' wakes. Note 'La Baleine' and her freedom rig

Florence Arthaud, sponsored by Biotherm skin cream but abandoned by good fortune. She eventually had to put in to the Azores

this time. There is a more important sight: outlined in the hatchway of his boat, looking out across the wheel, is the grey old lion himself. Tabarly has arrived. Quietly, a dozen cameras click on the dockside. 'Eric est là!'

Whatever is aerodynamically curved and technically perfect on *Paul Ricard* is square and stumpy and home-made on its neighbour, *Nord*. This is the Bulgarian: a folkboat, finished off without style, trailed overland across Europe by Vassil Kurtev, a former dentist to the Black Sea fishing fleet. Through a mouthful of fried chicken and a watchful interpreter called Markovsky, Kurtev is expounding his philosophy to me in the shabby little cabin. 'I do this for the spirit of the amateur, for my club and my country to promote friendship and sport.' His club, at Kavarna, raised money and had a rally to see him off. 'It was', says the interpreter, disconcertingly lapsing from the previous high rhetoric, 'really cute.' Homely curtains, a pine mirror, a tourist board medallion and another pile of chicken-bones give a homelike atmosphere. 'I have liked to meet the comrades from Canada, from America, the Dutch, the British.' Suddenly, abandoning his interpreter's services, Kurtev whips out a Russian edition of Val Howells' account of the 1960 race, fixes me with wild, pale green eyes, and translates:

'"We have a folkboat. It is not going to sink, rely on my words" – so writes the great Howells. I have a folkboat too. It is built by the reliable hands of my friends.' We shake hands, emotionally, and I clamber back onto the pontoon. 'A damn shame', says a passing sailor warmly, 'someone couldn't of put a few dollars into giving him a more solid boat.'

One more call to pay; at the far end of the pontoon, where *Ntombifuti*, 40 feet of Ed Dubois custom-built monohull, lies sleekly alongside *Quailo*. I am bitten by curiosity; the skipper is Ian Radford, who I last met in 1976, when he used the race to emigrate to America in *Jabulisiwe*, his little 28-footer, bought after he had worked in Zululand. He left as a junior doctor, and I felt that surely the rainbow's end must have worked out well for him to return unsponsored with this potential class winner. It had, but he was harassed. 'I'm alone. No help at all. No car. Can't even use the phones, all full of press, and every little thing is going wrong.' By Friday night, most problems solved, Ian is prepared to have a drink and reminisce.

'I loved the first race. A wonderful trip.' (This was in the roughest year, 1976; his little boat finished a creditable 39th, half-way down the fleet, ahead of bigger fish; he must be tough.) 'The next time, in 1980, I hated it, thought it was boring. Said "Oh God, what am I doing out here?"' But meanwhile he had become head of his department at the hospital in Miami, 'which paid for a boat

which might just win. Might be the first monohull home in her class.' Hence *Ntombifuti*, a tribute to old *Jabulisiwe*: it means, in Zulu, 'another girl'; the name traditionally given to a second daughter. Radford, blond-bearded, shy and abrupt, longs all week for the start, the peace, the end of the bustle. 'If you want to see me on the starting line', he says, 'look five minutes behind everyone else. I'm keeping well back. Last time a spectator boat rammed me and I did the whole race with no pulpit or lifelines.' I wished him, and his second daughter, all luck.

When you have come this far as a spectator and friend, living so close to the fleet huddled under its flags in the dock, it is difficult to realize that for you, left behind, nothing actually remains except a

'Biotherm II' being repaired under cover

windy morning, a motor boat trip around the harbour, and the sight of the fleet streaming out to sea. For them, it all lies ahead: for fragile red *City of Birmingham* under a cautiously reefed mainsail; for *Biotherm II*, repaired at last, though with flapping jib and fraught skipper; for serene little junk-rigged *Jester*; for jolly Bob Lengyel on *Prodigal*, shouting 'Nice ta be remembered!' to the cameramen who hung out of windows and planes; for big *Elf Aquitaine*, for *Fury* and *Fleury Michon*, both startling the commentators with dramatic spurts through the fleet on the starting line; for Tabarly and Jeantot and Phillips and Houlgrave, Mike and Chris and Bill and Vassil; for the stars and the dreamers, for 88 men and four women. In a sharp south-easterly they make westward along the coast; first the multihulls dissolve into the distance, then the main fleet eases away and disperses on the horizon. For two weeks or for seven, for one night or forever, each accepts the solitude and the sea. We turn back, grateful to get out of the biting wind.

*Three French entries in the 1984 race. From left,
Loick Peyron's catamaran 'Lada Poch', and
two trimarans: 'Kermarine' sailed by Vincent Levy
and Denis Gliksman's 'Lessive St Marc'*

FRANCIS CHICHESTER

LIMITED

DIRECTORS: FRANCIS CHICHESTER. S.M.CHICHESTER. M.COOPER

9 ST. JAMES'S PLACE, LONDON, S.W. 1

TEL: HYDE PARK 0931   GROSVENOR 8196

NAVIGATION SPECIALISTS

MAP MAKERS AND PUBLISHERS

2nd December, 1959.

George Everitt, Esq.,
Royal Western Yacht Club,
The Esplanade,
The Hoe,
Plymouth, Devon.

Dear Everitt,

        Hasler, who has originated the marvellous idea of a single
handed yacht race to New York, has written to your Vice
Commodore expressing the hope of the present Committee that
your club will handle the British end of the race.

        Plymouth seems to be the proper and traditional point of
departure for any race to America.

        Perhaps I feel more strongly about this as a Devonian!

        The Press and yachtsmen concerned seem to think that this
is likely to be the most sporting sailing event of the century
and I do hope that you will be in favour of handling the start.
One of the best national newspapers has offered to pay all the
expenses incurred by an organizing club, though I do not
believe that that would be an important inducement to the
Royal Western considering how they always handle the Fastnet
race.

        If I can give you any more information which you may need,
or if you would like to discuss the race, Hasler and I would be
very glad to visit you.

                        Yours sincerely,

                        Francis Chichester
                        FRANCIS CHICHESTER

P.S. I have just been talking to your cousin on the telephone.
He is only working half time at the Aero Club, but is in just
as good form as ever.

1960

It was as though the conquerors of Everest had set off for the summit equipped with no more than stout boots and a packet of peanut butter sandwiches. At 10 am on 11 June 1960 four small yachts pottered out of Plymouth and set sail for New York. As an event it was so low-key as to be scarcely worth noticing. Admittedly, there was one factor that had attracted a bit of attention: each of these little craft nosing off into the Atlantic had a crew of just one man aboard. But as individuals they were a modest lot: an ex-Marine, a map publisher, an East End doctor and a Welsh farmer. The Frenchman who set off five days late in the wake of this diminutive flotilla was no self-publicist either: formerly the assistant salad chef at New York's Waldorf-Astoria, his main purpose in joining the race was to deliver a boat – all 21 feet of it – to its American owner. Certainly none of these men would have chosen to think of themselves as laying out the course for what was to become the greatest singlehanded sailing race in the world. Two of them had packed their dinner jackets.

As a competitive encounter, the first Observer Singlehanded Transatlantic Race rather lacked the quality of urgency. (Twenty years later 62 yachts were to make the crossing in a faster time than the first winner.) One boat, having been forced off course to Bermuda, even stayed in harbour there for a couple of days so that her skipper could watch a cricket match.

But if the pace was leisurely, the challenge facing those early solo sailors was daunting. Self-steering gear was primitive and home-made. Roller-reefing was a pipe-dream. There were no satellites overhead to help with navigation – only pinpoint stars in a wildly tossing sky: even the route across the ocean had to be chosen with only the sketchiest precedents to guide them.

For those seeking comfort and fair winds there was the old square rigger route dog-legging down to the Canaries to benefit from the trade winds, or the slightly shorter option of going south-west to the Azores, then across to New York. The first three home in 1960 opted for variations of the more direct Great Circle and Rhumb Line routes, risking fog and ice to the north and the powerful westerly currents of the Gulf Stream to the south of them in order to reduce the distance to just under 3,000 miles. All the winning competitors since then have followed in their wakes.

Francis Chichester and Blondie Hasler and the rest showed the way; they proved it could be done. All came through the ordeal unassisted. They demonstrated that even a tiny sailing boat, properly equipped, could outbrave the Atlantic. They baptized an item of equipment – self-steering gear – which in its own way has become as important to the offshore sailor as the compass and the sextant.

And the 1960 race did something else. It began to chart the outlines of a map unknown to most navigators, but to which every new singlehanded sailor turns with anxiety and hope: the map of a mind alone, at sea, and constantly at risk. In the midst of the screeching, drumming din of a 100mph storm Chichester had recorded simply: 'I am flogged to the bone.' But when he sighted land at last he wrote in his diary: 'I quite understand why people used to, and still do, go into retreat. During a month alone I think at last you become a real person and are concerned with the real value of life.'

Left: Chichester's persuasive letter to the RWYC urging them to take on the race

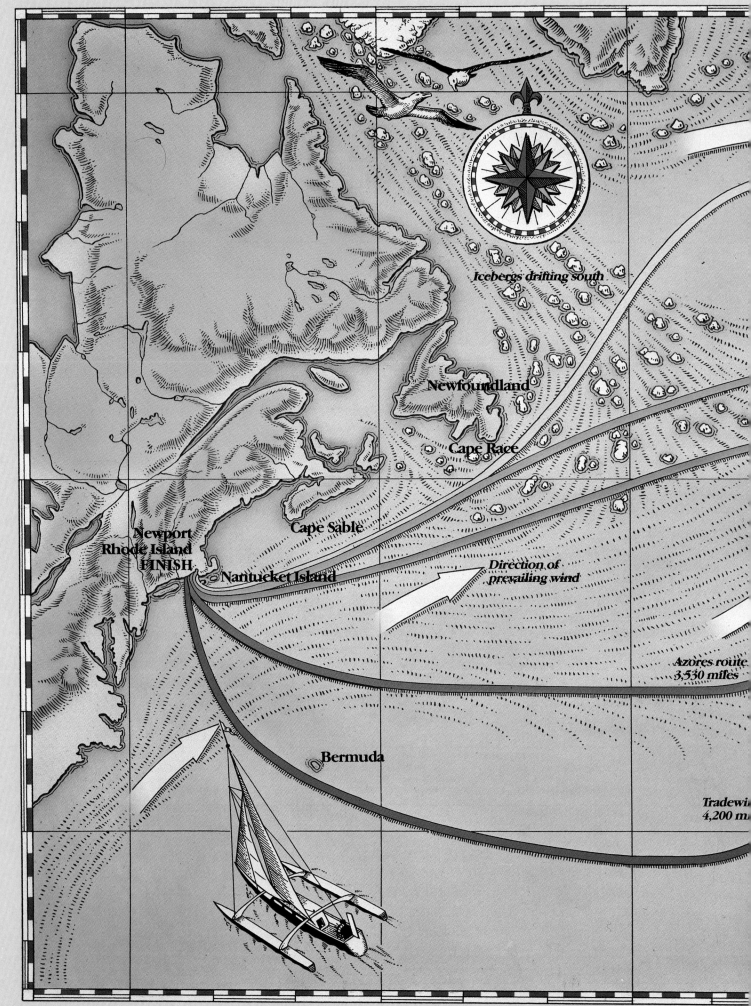

Icebergs drifting south

Newfoundland

Cape Race

Cape Sable

Newport
Rhode Island
FINISH

Nantucket Island

Direction of
prevailing wind

Azores route
3,530 miles

Bermuda

Tradewi
4,200 m

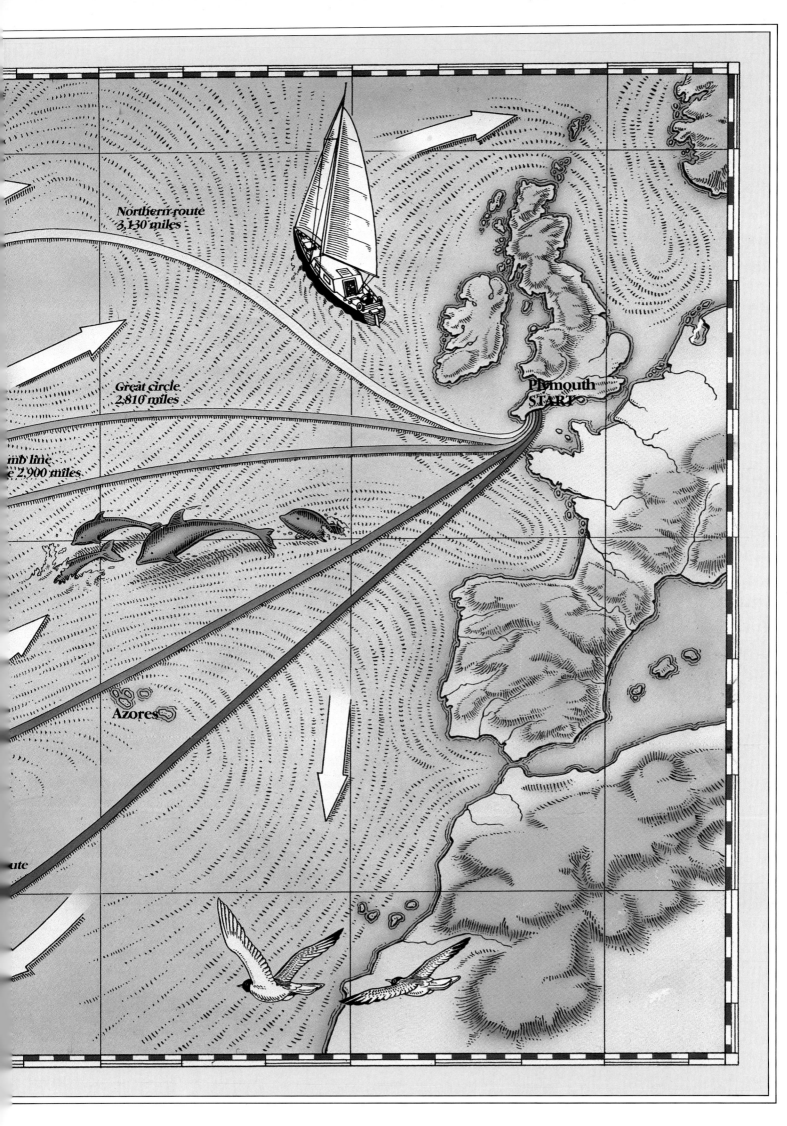

Northern route
3,130 miles

Great circle
2,810 miles

mb line
e 2,900 miles.

Azores

ute

Plymouth
START

A quarter of a century ago the very idea seemed utter folly, a madcap stunt. It would be dangerous. It would attract infinitesimal public interest. Besides, it would be illegal. Today there are those who treat sailing the Atlantic singlehanded as a sprint. Back in 1960, however, it required persistence and persuasiveness to get the world's first solo ocean race – from Plymouth to New York – under way. *The Observer*'s former sports editor Christopher Brasher was closely involved and some years later wrote this account of the birth of OSTAR.

HOW IT ALL BEGAN

Christopher Brasher

'In the winter, I studied my Atlantic Ocean racing in the Round Pond at Kensington Gardens, where I went every Sunday morning for a short time and watched the model boys. I figured that if they could sail a model across the Round Pond without a helmsman, I could sail my yacht across the Atlantic in the same way.'

'I hoped to get a time that would be difficult to beat. But every time I tried to point 'Gipsy Moth' at New York the wind blew dead on the nose. It was like trying to reach a doorway with a man in it aiming a hose at you. It was much tougher than I thought.'

Sir Francis Chichester

We were worried as we took the train down to Plymouth. There were four of us, eating a British Rail lunch and plotting our strategy: Lt.-Col. H. G. Hasler, usually known as 'Blondie'; Francis Chichester, whom Blondie had introduced to the Editor of *The Observer* as 'a friend of mine who runs a map publishing business in St James's'; Lindley Abbatt, then the paper's promotions manager, and myself, at that time sports editor.

We had to try to persuade some gentlemen from the Royal Western Yacht Club that it would be a good idea if they acted as organizers of the first-ever singlehanded transatlantic race sailed from east to west. We did not have much hope. Up to that time almost the entire yachting establishment had rejected the idea. It was too unconventional, and besides it broke one of the fundamental rules of the sea – that the crew of a vessel under way should at all times be keeping watch.

We need not have worried. As we sat down around a table in the headquarters of the Royal Western on Plymouth Hoe, Lt.-Col. Jack Odling-Smee, the club's rear commodore, opened the proceedings with the question: 'At what date and time would you like to start, gentlemen?'

Left: The famous four. Clockwise: Francis Chichester, Blondie Hasler, David Lewis, Val Howells.
Five days later, former salad chef Jean Lacombe tagged on to the tiny fleet

And so, on 11 June 1960, at 10 o'clock in the morning, four competitors – 'very gallant gentlemen' – set sail from Plymouth harbour with the following instructions: 'Cross the starting line from west to east, leaving the Melampus buoy to starboard, then to New York by any route.'

The simplicity of those instructions was fundamental to the concept and remains so to this day – despite some refinements governing the seaworthiness and size of vessels and the number of entrants.

That concept was Blondie Hasler's.

Invalided out of the Royal Marines in 1948 with a spinal complaint, Blondie bought a boat in which he lived during winter and cruised during summer. It wasn't long before he decided that all the rigging and cordage on a modern yacht puts it at about the same stage of development as the Wright brothers' aeroplane. So in 1953 he built himself a Scandinavian folkboat and called it *Jester* – 'because it is going to be such a bloody joke.' He experimented with it until he had perfected an extremely simple Chinese lugsail. Basically it needs only two controlling ropes – one to hoist the sail, the other to control the angle of the sail to the wind. It has no cockpit – only a circular hatch protected by a hood from which you can do everything. It is so simple that even I felt, after half an hour at the tiller, that I could sail it to America.

It took Blondie six years – from 1953 to 1959 – to get *Jester*'s rig right. Halfway through he decided he needed to test his ideas, and his mind turned to 'the most difficult "up-hill" course I could think of – across the North Atlantic against the prevailing winds.' Francis Chichester crystallizes the thought in one sentence: 'I believe that this is the greatest urge to adventure for a man – to have an idea, an ideal or an ambition, and then to prove, at any cost, that the idea is right, or that the ambition can be fulfilled.'

Blondie's first attempt to interest *The Observer* failed, but by 1957 he had the support of the Slocum Society – devoted to the memory of Captain Joshua Slocum, first man to sail alone round the world. A press release was issued, and Blondie pinned a copy, dated 21 September 1957, to the noticeboard at the Royal Ocean Racing Club headquarters. As a result, Francis Chichester was to become the most famous lone yachtsman in the world.

Francis at this time was extremely ill. Five different doctors had given the same verdict – 'cancer of the lung'. His office in St James's was just around the corner from the club's headquarters, and Francis called in there on his way to hospital for what he believed was a farewell drink with friends. As he left, he saw Blondie's notice, and thought:

'Jester' skippered by Hasler in 1960 and 1964

'That would be a terrific race.' By 1959, when Francis was sufficiently recovered to be able to get about, the race was still in his mind. Blondie had acquired an ally.

By now he had rekindled the interest of *The Observer* through an old friend of his, another ex-Royal Marine named David Astor – who conveniently happened to be Editor.

The race became essentially a friendly amateur affair – a bit hare-brained, and eccentric in the best

traditions of British sport. Nobody has explained it better than Francis Chichester in his autobiography *The Lonely Sea and the Sky*. He is describing his fourth week at sea during the first race:

'I came to terms with life. I found that my sense of humour had returned; things which would have irritated me or maddened and infuriated me ashore made me laugh out loud, and I dealt with them steadily and efficiently. Rain, fog, gale, squalls, and turbulent forceful seas under grey skies became merely obstacles. I seemed to have found the true values of life. The meals I

*Chichester's 'Gipsy Moth III', first OSTAR winner
and the biggest boat in the race*

cooked myself were feasts, and my noggins of
whisky were nectar. A good sleep was as valuable
to me as the Koh-i-noor diamond. All my senses
seemed to be sharpened. I was enjoying life, and
treating it as it should be treated – lightly.
Tackling tough jobs gave me a wonderful sense
of achievement and pleasure.'

There were seven entrants in 1960. Four were
British: Hasler, Chichester, David Lewis – a small
curly-haired doctor from the East End of London –
and Val Howells, a Welsh giant with a flowing black
beard, a deep voice, and a crunching handshake.

There was a small and rubbery Frenchman, Jean
Lacombe, who got off five days late in a tiny
plywood boat, the 21ft *Cap Horn*. An American,
Arthur Piver, took so long getting his trimaran
across the Atlantic via the Azores that he never
started. A German named Karminski sent an entry
form but was never heard of again.

After the excitement of the start, news became
very scarce. Each boat had a radio with which it

could transmit messages for short distances, and we had an arrangement with Pan American that their pilots would listen on the right frequency as they flew over the Atlantic. But for two weeks we heard nothing. Eventually Val Howells in *Eira* was sighted by a German vessel on the direct route to the Azores. Then the Cunard liner *Mauretania* sighted Chichester in *Gipsy Moth III*; a day later a British cargo vessel sighted Hasler in *Jester*. They were both in mid-Atlantic, with *Gipsy Moth* at 37 degrees 38 minutes West – neck-and-neck after nearly three weeks.

A week later Francis transmitted a message to Cape Race radio in Newfoundland and *The Observer* carried the headline: YACHTSMAN SAILS 2,100 MILES FROM PLYMOUTH IN 27 DAYS. No names – in those days Chichester was unknown.

I flew to New York to join his wife Sheila. A report came in that he had been sighted off Nantucket, and I went down to the East River and hired a tiny Piper Cub. We flew up the coast of Long Island and down again, but never far from land because the pilot was a cautious man. Next day I obtained a plane with floats and searched the sea again. Still no sign of Francis. By now stories were starting to appear in the press: LONE YACHTSMAN MISSING. But eventually a message came through that coastguards had sighted Chichester. Two press colleagues and I chartered an amphibious plane and flew out over the skyscrapers. And there she was, a trim and beautiful yacht alone on the ocean, in sight of journey's end.

Chichester had taken 40 days, 12 hours and 30 minutes for the crossing – a time which many experts thought fantastic. Hasler came in second after 48 days.

To the second man in any race goes little glory. But to Blondie Hasler, who passed the Ambrose Lightship off New York at 3.30 am on 30 July, the mere fact that he had completed the course without mishap was a cause of immense satisfaction.

When the yellow-painted, junk-rigged *Jester*, with Hasler's pinkish-brown bald head peering out from under the white pram canopy that protects the central hatch, sailed into New York harbour, he had effectively proved the soundness of his theories about yacht design and equipment. The race – his race – had done what he had hoped it could.

Perhaps the most amazing fact about his journey was that for the whole 48 days, with the sole exception of one hour, *Jester* steered herself. The only time that Hasler took the tiller was for an hour when he was near the Longships off Land's End with heavy seas running. 'This has been a tremendous satisfaction to me,' he said, 'as this steering gear has been one of my chief babies.'

His second baby – the single Chinese lugsail on an unstayed mast – also flourished. Not once did he have to go on deck during bad weather, and yet he kept *Jester* sailing near her maximum whatever the wind. 'The strength of the wind goes up and down like a yo-yo in the Atlantic, and I sometimes had to reef or unreef 20 times in 24 hours.'

But he did all this very simply with the aid of two Terylene ropes, about the size of a pyjama cord, which come to the central hatch.

There could not, in fact, have been a greater contrast between his voyage and that of Francis Chichester.

To use Hasler's own analogy about the design of a modern yacht, it is as if Chichester had been driving a large car, and every time he wanted to change gear (increase or decrease his sail area) he had to stop, get out and jack up the rear wheels and fit two new wheels (from a store of wheels on the back seat) of a different diameter, remove the jacks, get in and drive off again.

Hasler, by contrast, stood under his pram canopy, adjusted two ropes, and the sail became the size that he wanted. He said that his object was to design a rig that would enable a 16-year-old girl to cruise anywhere safely by herself. And he did it.

Hasler had a placid and unadventurous passage, except for 'a lousy bit of navigation near Ireland'. On the fifth day out of Plymouth he obtained one sun sight, and he believed this rather than his dead-reckoning position. Visibility was only a quarter of a mile when he heard the Fastnet fog-gun going off.

He believed that he was well clear of it and lay down to rest. There wasn't much wind and the ship was close-hauled on the port tack when she suddenly put herself about. Hasler popped his head through the hatch, and 400 yards away was the base of a rocky coast with its head in the mist.

'*Jester* and Spencer must have decided that they didn't want to hit Ireland, so they tacked.' Spencer was a yellow rubber poodle given to him before he left by Cynthia Major, the wife of Ian Major, the first person to design a self-steering gear of the sort used by Hasler. Spencer sat by one of the small forward portholes, 'always on watch'.

Besides Spencer, Hasler had the almost constant company of a fulmar and sometimes a great shearwater – a species of bird that only breeds on Tristan da Cunha. 'My private fulmar is escorting me,' he wrote in his log, 'flying around, settling or chasing me. She has just settled five yards in front of my bow and then pretended to be greatly alarmed when I nearly ran her down.'

After the first week, when he was seasick twice, he ate well. His log read: 'I think I am eating too much and taking no exercise.' Breakfast consisted of an apple or orange, then porridge, sometimes raw with milk and some sultanas.

Little 'Jester', one of the five contestants in 1960, sets off at the start of the 1964 race, dwarfed by some of the spectator boats

Lunch was always cold. Crispbread and cheese, a glass of wine and dates. He had a cup of tea in the afternoon and then cooked supper – a stew or a rice dish. The stews were made of potatoes, onions, carrots and salt beef, which Hasler kept in a two-gallon polythene jar and fished out with a piece of bent wire.

'Really, I found I was jolly busy. Even washing up takes three-quarters of an hour when the ship is pitching and I did a lot of carpentry – this table, those shelves and lights.' When he ran out of crispbread he made his own bread, grinding the wheat in a coffee grinder and mixing it with sea water, 'which has just the right amount of salt in it.'

He had one long gale of three days, which was 'a bit of a bore', but he always managed to keep some sail on her. And then there came a golden day after the storm.

'It is getting dark and she is bounding along on a broad reach throwing up cascades of water on either bow as she dips into the backs of the waves every few moments. I have turned the hood so that its open side faces forward, and I stand after a hot supper with a full belly and a glass of wine in my hand, revelling in the way she goes. This is what *I* came for.'

Val Howells, who had had to put in to Bermuda for some repairs, arrived after 63 days and said: 'Never again! I wouldn't so much as cross the bloody Serpentine in the *Queen Mary!*' Half an hour later, sitting in the cockpit of *Eira* as she was towed into Sheepshead Bay, he said: 'You know, for the *next* singlehanded race I'm thinking of trying a schooner....'

Little Jean Lacombe delivered the tiny *Cap Horn* to its new owner in New York after a crossing of 74 days. He still holds the record – for the slowest OSTAR passage.

1964

The Observer Singlehanded was a precocious race right from the start. A mere four years after it had found its infant sealegs and ambled happily across the Atlantic, little OSTAR had grown into a strapping, highly ambitious adolescent. 1964 was the second time the event had been held. But in some important respects it was a maiden voyage. For the first time the fleet included a boat that had been specially designed for an east-to-west singlehanded Atlantic crossing – Eric Tabarly's ketch *Pen Duick II*. For the first time the line-up, now swollen to 15 starters, began to take on a properly international flavour, with a Dane and an Australian competing as well as Tabarly and second-timer Jean Lacombe from France. This was also the race that introduced the multihullers to the perils of big seas, contrary winds and the attendant fears of a capsize far from land.

It was exactly as Lt.-Col. Hasler had planned. The whole point of the race was to encourage experiment and resourcefulness, to inspire the development of 'boats that were not only seaworthy, fast and weatherly, but also comfortable and exceptionally easy to handle'. How big (and therefore fast) could a boat be without overtaxing the resources of her all-in-one skipper, crew, navigator and cook? That was what the race was designed to discover, and that was the question to which the 1964 race began to supply the answers.

To Hasler's delight, it was the bespoke boat, *Pen Duick*, that was first across the line at Newport, Rhode Island, the finish having been moved there from New York for navigational reasons. What was more, Tabarly had done most of the trip with his self-steering out of action. 'The boat was designed and built on a very small budget,' wrote Hasler happily, 'and Eric's performance in getting her to the Brenton Reef in 27 days, in spite of an unserviceable steering gear, must rank very near the summit of singlehanded sailing.' (So thought *le tout France* also, whose enthusiasm for the Breton's victory that year rapidly grew into a nationwide passion for the sport, whose dedicated followers have invaded Millbay Dock for every Transatlantic Race since then in growing numbers.)

What further impressed Hasler and confounded the head-shaking greybeards back in the sailing club bar-rooms at home was that all three multihulls – a trimaran and two cats – had completed the voyage safely. Even so, recalling a rogue wave that had once put his own tough little *Jester* on her side off Aberdeen, he was not absolutely convinced: 'With further development,' he predicted cautiously, 'a multihuller may possibly be able to win, although my own guess is that the single-huller, given comparable development, will always do better in hard going and rough weather.'

That sentence must bring a wry smile to the old seadog's jowls today. From 1964 the story of OSTAR was to take on a distinctly dual personality. On the one hand it was to remain – and always will remain – a test of individual seamanship and courage, applying equally to the skippers of the smallest family cruisers as to the hard men on their giant racing machines. On the other it had begun to evolve into a very special kind of contest, between high tech and the high seas.... These days the designers are out there too, ghostly presences on the foredeck, with their eyes on the rigging and their hearts in their mouths.

Left: Francis Chichester handling sail aboard 'Gipsy Moth'. The headgear was a trade mark

47

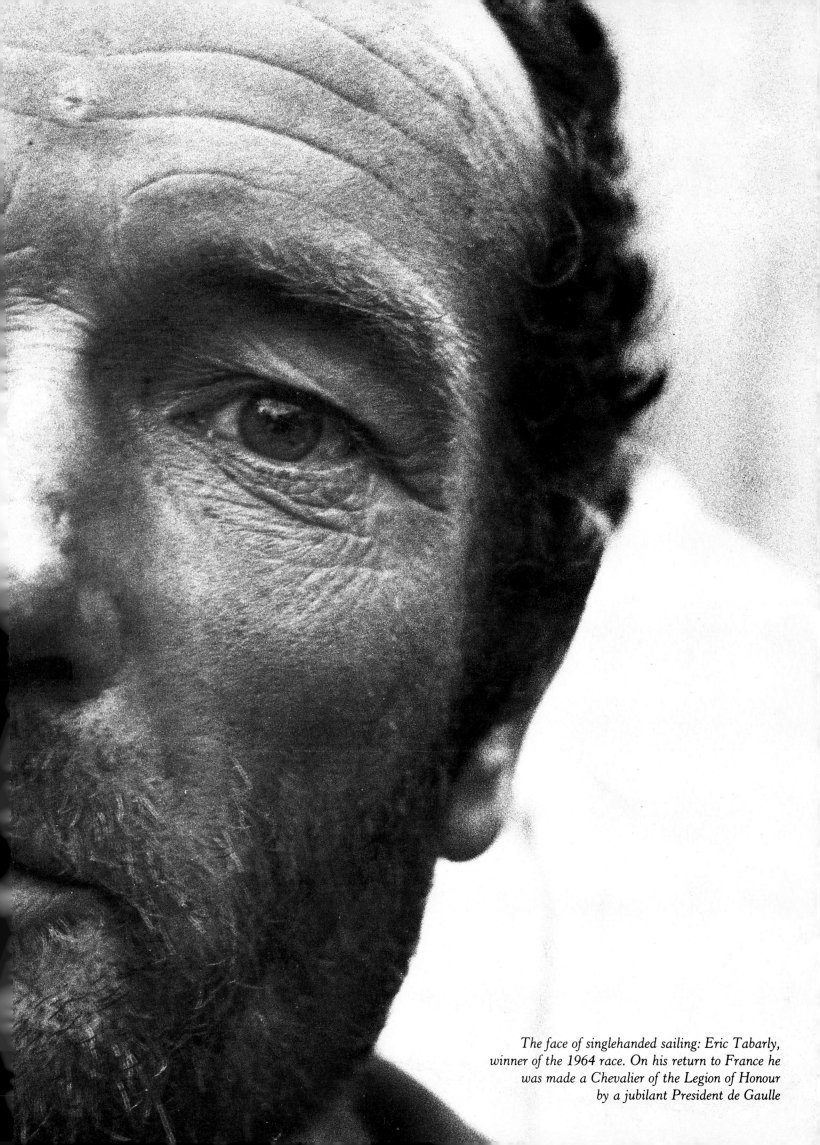

The face of singlehanded sailing: Eric Tabarly,
winner of the 1964 race. On his return to France he
was made a Chevalier of the Legion of Honour
by a jubilant President de Gaulle

A great many column inches have appeared in the world's press about the Observer Singlehanded Transatlantic Race, mainly written by yachting correspondents. In 1964, however, *The Guardian's* star American correspondent decided to report on the finish of the second OSTAR. Newport, Rhode Island is only a few hours' drive from New York and Alistair Cooke was there to file this report back to England, datelined 19 June. The headline was: 'Tabarly beats record by five days: Three weeks without any proper sleep.'

TABARLY'S TRIUMPH

Alistair Cooke

At four minutes to ten this morning, a chic 45ft ketch with a black plywood hull, and a dinky upside down yellow lifeboat attached, skimmed between Brenton Reef and the reef light tower here, and a slight tremor was recorded on Nelson's Column in Trafalgar Square.

A Frenchman had attempted, and what is worse achieved, the audacity of crossing the Atlantic in 27 days, 1 hour and 56 minutes, or better than five days under Chichester's 1962 (non-OSTAR) record. Not to fiddle around with the awful truth, ladies and gentlemen, a Breton rules the waves!

He is Eric Tabarly, a 32-year-old lieutenant in the French Navy, a curly brown-haired, brown-bearded, merry-eyed, compact little man of Napoleonic (5ft 4in) stature, but with the wide-eyed insouciance of Jean Pierre Belmondo giving the slip to French Customs or blowing up Brasilia. According to a close friend of his, panting for the great reunion as we plunged into a heavy sea towards the reef, Tabarly had two ambitions in life: to cross the Atlantic singlehanded and to 'fight the English'.

'*Comment?* Fight?'

'Yes – to attack, to defeat perhaps?'

'Ah, to beat?'

'Yes – to beat the English, no?'

'Yes.'

He had done it, and when we spotted his graceful 'Swallow' ('*pen duick*' is Breton for the bird) coming over the horizon into a 12mph south-west wind we must say that we also saw at our elbow an ecstatic white-haired French Consul from Boston, and one Captain Chatel, a naval attaché, strutting on the balls of his feet, and a French correspondent pointing with dramatic emphasis to a headline in *Le Monde*: '*Tabarly serait en tête des solitaires.*'

Tabarly was, without doubt, the leader of the singlehanders. As the French captain put it: 'We cannot understand why we should be winning, and

the British cannot understand why they should be losing. It is historic, and it is very droll.'

It was droller than we knew, for Tabarly told us that for the whole month at sea he had no idea whether he was winning or losing until seven this morning, when a couple of yachts and a young outboarder went out to greet him and conveyed, by grotesque sign language, that he was indeed *numéro un*. Tabarly had a radio, but he tried once to reach a French station, failed, and switched it off for good. '*Le TSF*,' he said. 'I do not like.'

'Offhand' is the word that the French aboard used to pinpoint the character of the Bretons. 'And is he Breton?' the friend said. 'Typical, a comical character. They don't give a damn.'

We expected him some time last evening, but at seven o'clock he was reported 74 miles from the finishing line and buffeting west-north-west winds up to eight knots. This made it impossible for him to do much more than five knots through the night. Then the wind swivelled round to south-west, and suddenly the coastguard reported him 'right off Point Judith and going like crazy.'

When we caught up with him, we and a score of yachts, outboards, put-puts, and fire-boats streaming jets of water in salute, he was ambling in with slack sails towards the harbour and looking up with red eyes to jumping-jack photographers bawling without success, to 'Wave, man, wave!'

At last, he was tied up to the Port o'Call Marina, and several thousand Americans in a hundred variations of the colourful native summer costume straddled the rails and stanchions and peered down at the little bobbing black hull flying the Tricolor; for he was hemmed in by the contestants in tomorrow's record entry for the Newport-Bermuda race, no fewer than 145 yachts of indescribable splendour, a concentration of nautical wealth that must have been very awesome to a Breton lad who wouldn't think of going home any other way than

he came. ('Naturally, I will sail back alone, it is my own boat, it would cost money to ship it.')

The characterization of Bretons as 'offhand' took on a stoical grandeur when we got him in to port. A score or more newsmen jumped aboard and scuffed the decks and bruised the paint and cracked a spar or two. He paid no heed. He stood there in a blue navy jersey and blue slacks and happily answered all questions in two languages and several dialects.

What was the worst trouble? Like Chichester and every other veteran, the answer was the same: the lack of any prolonged sleep. On the eighth day he broke the governor shaft of his automatic steerer, and from then on he had to steer by hand.

The weather, though, was better than he had hoped. Gales on three days, once the winds went to Force 9. Still, he had never expected to do it in under 30 days.

His course was just south of the Great Circle, and although he was becalmed a couple of times, he was never frustrated by the winds, and the fog never lasted very long, so he stayed with it. He didn't seem to suffer, ever, from Chichester's chronic bellyache about which leg to take. He did what came naturally. He ate rice, spaghetti, a little tinned meat, and had lots of red wine.

'Swallow' was designed specially for this race. She has a very deep keel and is very light, perhaps half as heavy as a normal ketch of her size. The hull is 12mm plywood. He has no complaints about it at all. He would like to do it all again.

Was there any special ordeal? He apparently had never heard the word. But, after coaching by the more intense reporters, he got the idea. The worst thing, he said, was the nightmares that come from broken sleep. He said it with a chuckle, as if he were describing an unexpected bonus.

As he was led away to the mayor and a reception committee, to receive the seal of the city and the yacht club's tie-clip ('in case he ever wears a tie'), the French friend swelled up like a pouter pigeon. 'This, you understand', he said, 'is an entirely new sport in France. Five years ago very bad results in the Channel race. Ten years ago, nothing. Now – mon Dieu – the sale of boats to young Frenchmen, it will be sensationnel, sensationnel!'

Tabarly aboard 'Pen Duick II': his ambition was 'to fight the English'. He also succeeded in inspiring the French

'Folatre', 35ft, Derek Kelsall

'Ilala', 38ft, Mike Ellison

'Akka', 35ft, Val Howells

'Ericht', 31ft, Geoffrey Chaffey

'Tammy Norie', 40ft, Robin McCurdy

'Rehu Moana', 40ft, David Lewis

'Stardrift', 30ft, Bill Howell

'Vanda Caelea', 25ft, Bob Bunker

1968

The Observer Singlehanded Trans-atlantic Race came of age in 1968. With the arrival of commercial sponsorship it could be said to have begun earning its keep – at least in the case of the most ambitious competitors. It was also the year when a race which so far had been an all-male event had its first encounter with the opposite sex. It turned out to be an unhappy one: Edith Baumann, a German secretary who entered a 39ft trimaran, sank just a few days out in the Bay of Biscay and had to be rescued, along with her dog Schatz (another first for OSTAR).

The start itself, however, had been a placid affair. Thirty-five boats crossed the line, more than half of them from overseas. But this great gathering of the world's most audacious solo sailors provided a rather dismal spectacle: there was scarcely a breath of wind, and it was raining. The publicity men from the Scotch whisky firm and the brewery and the importers of Italian sparkling wine who were among the event's novice sponsors that year must have felt an anxious sense of anticlimax.

In fact, drama was not long in overtaking the fleet. Edith Baumann's *Koala III* was not the only casualty in a race that convincingly underlined the hazards of singlehanded sailing. Nearly half those who had ghosted away from Plymouth on 1 June never finished. There were dismastings and sink-ings and broken rudders.

The most startling victim was Eric Tabarly, the winner in 1964 and by now a convert to the multihull cause. To those who thought such craft unacceptably experimental a French supporter had retorted: 'Ha! Eric could win the race at 20 knots on a piece of bread.' In the event, his 67ft trimaran *Pen Duick IV* ripped into an anchored freighter at 15

knots early in the race, set off again later after repairs, but then developed steering problems and had to retire.

Had Tabarly stayed the course, it might easily have been the first year in which a multihuller won. As it turned out, it was a big, strong monohulled yacht – with the aid of a weather-forecasting computer back in London – that was first in past the Brenton Tower. Geoffrey Williams's ketch *Sir Thomas Lipton* was able to skirt the gale that had everyone else lying a-hull in screaming winds and fierce seas and thus taught singlehanders another lesson about the value of new technology applied to an old predicament.

Another boat escaped the gale – the American proa *Cheers* – by taking the long route via the Azores. She came in third, not only clinching the case for unorthodox hull configurations but giving new life to the great bar-room debate about the advantages (or otherwise) of the southerly option.

Nevertheless, it was Williams who won the victor's laurels that year; and it was his backers, suppliers of Lipton's tea, who set the pace for the great sponsorship contests that were now to follow. Soon French face cream would be racing against Japanese cars, and luffing duels would ensue between champagne and a dehydrated pea.

Left: Leslie Williams's 'Spirit of Cutty Sark'

SIR THOMAS LIPTON

Faces of '68
Top left:
Flanking
winner Geoffrey
Williams are
the American
Tom Follett,
left, and the
South African
Bruce Dalling

Top right:
'Sir Thomas
Lipton' is seen
here showing
her paces
with Skipper
Williams
enjoying the
luxury of
a proper crew

Bottom row,
left to right:
Ake Matteson
finished 18th
in 'Goodwin II'
but was
disqualified,
Marc Cuilinski
of 'Abrima'
which sank,
Eric Williams
who skippered
'Coila' and had
to retire when he
became ill, and
the Rev. Stephen
Pakenham of
'Rob Roy' who
finished 15th,
in 42 days

As the Observer Singlehanded Transatlantic Race gathered momentum so it began to attract bigger and faster entries. They were also more expensive than the first fairly conventional cruising craft. Where was the money to build these specially designed yachts to come from? How could skippers afford the time to familiarize themselves with their boats and complete their qualifying sails as well as taking part in the race? Enter the sponsors – to the disgust of the yachting establishment, but to the benefit of yachting itself.

A MESSAGE FROM OUR SPONSORS

Libby Purves

One of the oddest sights at the London Boat Show in January 1977 was of a powerful 38ft yacht propped on its great keel, around which roared the Hoovers of the last-minute cleaning ladies. A shoal of press and television cameramen, trailing wires and popping flashbulbs, crowded beneath her bow like surf; and above their heads a slight, elegant woman smiled down from the deck, one arm thrown matily around a giant gollywog. At a table nearby, a group of public-relations people smiled even more broadly. The boat was *Robertson's Golly*; the woman was Clare Francis; and the sponsors, James Robertson & Co., were busy getting more than their money's worth. In one of the toughest years of a tough race, a pretty girl had steered their woolly black symbol across 3,000 miles of ocean to finish 13th out of a fleet of 124 and take the trophy for the first woman home. And in return for modest financial support for her boat, here she was arm-in-arm with a man in a golly suit, smiling for the press and covering their jams with reflected glory in every television interview. It was a coup. Sponsorship in OSTAR had come of age.

Things may not have seemed so rosy, of course, in the PR offices of Gauloises cigarettes, Kriter wines and Pronuptia lingerie (whose namesake boat, festooned in dainty underthings, had raised the blood pressure of conservative yacht club elders in Millbay Dock before the start). For *Kriter III* broke up and sank, *Gauloises* sprang a leak and took that product name inexorably to the sea-bed, and *Pronuptia*, with fearful irony, suffered sail problems and retired from the race 'with its knickers', as one elder unkindly put it, 'in a right old twist'. *Kriter*, it should be fairly said, bounced back in 1980 with its name on no fewer than three boats, including Dame Naomi James's *Kriter Lady*, and won three good places; the ill-fated cigarettes, however, also tried again with Eric Loizeau's *Gauloises IV*, which was holed in the hull and retired. There is nothing safe about investing your promotional budget and your name in a racing boat. 'You cast your bread upon

the waters,' as one sponsor thoughtfully remarked, 'and watch it float away.' Often forever.

The story of the sponsors who have gambled on individual boats and skippers in the singlehanded race makes a fascinating counterpoint to its history. In the beginning there was resistance, horrified old-school yachting resistance, to the very idea. D. H. Clarke (author of *An Evolution of Singlehanders*) was asked for his opinion at the start of the race. He recognized early that commercial money would probably be needed to support it, and wrote:

'If an event such as this becomes popular – which

Above: Clare Francis, by 'Golly'. Opposite: Chris Smith's 1984 entry

I very much doubt – it won't be long before the Atlantic is cluttered from shore to shore with floating hoardings advertising just about any-thing.... Bloody floating ads, promoted and sponsored by money-greedy Big Businesses, are *not*, in my opinion, yachts.'

The Royal Western Yacht Club disagreed. When the third race opened in 1968, Rule 8 stated tersely that:

'Entries may be sponsored and/or financed by another person, body, or organization.'

And so began a policy which the secretary of the club, Commander Lloyd Foster, describes as 'bene-volent and liberal towards sponsored boats'. Not everyone agrees with it, even now, 'but we have to have them. You can't turn the clock back'.

The beginning was amateurish and low-key enough for anyone. One of the first sponsored skippers was Leslie Williams, in *Spirit of Cutty Sark*. 'Our whisky', says John Rudd, then and now managing director of Berry Bros. & Rudd, 'was not very well known then. The race was a new thing

*'Travacrest Seaway',
Peter Phillips's powerful
trimaran: sponsored by
the makers of fully
integrated autopilot
control systems. Her
earlier name, when she
was sponsored by a West
Country garage chain,
was 'Livery Dole'*

too, which is why we did it. It was the right time.'
The firm made a substantial contribution to the cost
of finishing the boat, and – Mr Rudd being a
yachtsman himself – offered advice and moral
support. 'I suppose we may have been able to
remind him about one or two things he ought to
take . . . in fact, we may have got a bit carried away,
what with the excitement, having the Royal
Marines band at the launching and so forth. Still, it
did create a bit of a stir.'

Compared to modern sponsorship, it was all very

hesitant and gentlemanly. And 'no, not a frightfully
good investment I suppose. We never really
calculated much.' John Rudd flew to Newport to
wait for the boat, and welcome Leslie Williams: 'He
didn't win, though. Pity.' Looking at the big
sponsors now, who may lay out half a million on an
experimental trimaran, Mr Rudd is definite in his
views. 'I think they're a bunch of lunatics.' *Spirit of
Cutty Sark*, incidentally, later changed her name to
Express Crusader and took Naomi James around the
world; later still, she became *Kriter Lady* in the 1980

OSTAR: full circle. The Royal Western places no impediment to such changes; there is no rule that a yacht must race under its original registered name.

Indeed, as the rule book evolves through the successive races, the attitude of the club can be appreciated as extraordinarily responsive to new twists in the sponsorship business; always keeping a jump ahead of the threatened excesses. By 1972 they felt it necessary to extend the terse Rule 8 (by now Rule 9):

'... The Royal Western Yacht Club of England are not averse to the sponsorship of entries and are indeed glad of the help that has been given to the competitors in the previous Races, which undoubtedly added to the interest in them. Nevertheless they are concerned that this race should remain a sporting event and reserve the right to refuse an entry if it appears that the primary object of it is to promote a commercial project not connected with the object of the race.'

This statement has remained central to the rules ever since. It means, explains Lloyd Foster, that a boat disguised as a beer bottle for no good reason would be frowned upon. Further, controls were brought in on 'emblems or wording' on sails or hull; and the boat's name must be a name (like *Bloggs' Emulsion*) and not a slogan (like *Bloggs' keeps you regular*).

The committee, quite clearly anticipating trouble, reserved 'the right to reject a name which they consider to be offensive or distasteful'; but fortunately, no such tasteless company has yet come forward with such a thing.

By 1980 company logos were allowed, of modest size, to be carried only on the hull. Spinnakers remain a problem, since yachts carry several, and tend to get themselves widely photographed in advance with their enormous advertisements flying, only to take these meekly down and bag them up while under the eagle eye of the starters and scrutineers. Size of lettering is laid down also; and names restricted to 20 characters. *Serta Perfectsleeper* and *Spirit of Cutty Sark* have just made it. Finally, as a 1984 refinement of the Royal Western policy of flexible cunning:

'Where publicity for a yacht's sponsors is obtained by an entry in the race, for example by the name of the yacht, an additional "sponsored entry fee" of £300 will be payable.'

At a rough computation, this should bring in an extra £6,000 to £7,000. Canny management.

For after all, to the really big Class I sponsors, £300 is barely more than a routine press lunch. 'We're entering an era now,' says Commander Lloyd Foster, 'where skippers of really big sponsored boats have virtually formed a union ... the French, some of them, are advocating money

'VSD': *sponsored by a French magazine in 1980*

prizes, even *appearance money* like tennis players.' We have not reached that pass yet; but the club knows perfectly well which century it is living in, and trims its sails admirably to the prevailing winds. It has not forgotten Hasler's early dream; the man on his own, who has sold his car for a new suit of sails, is as welcome as the oil company's lushest protégé; and doesn't have to pay the extra fee.

What I suspect will always preserve OSTAR is not only the club's vigilance, but the sheer riskiness of the enterprise. It was never easy to find a sporting sponsor and it is no easier now; in her book, *Come Hell or High Water*, Clare Francis wrote:

'I am quite sure that many companies have a file marked "Nutters", and that my request for sponsorship went into it. It's a feeling one got from their replies, which had the patient tone of a parent explaining to a child that unfortunately there are no sweeties to be had today ... at least one company said they couldn't believe that a little thing like me could possibly manage to cross the Atlantic alone, and they would not like to encourage me to do so.'

Clare Francis was not even looking for total sponsorship. She had been lent a boat, and merely needed equipment, modifications and provisioning. But in a sport where one small stainless steel shackle can cost £15, and a radio transmitter several thousand pounds, she inevitably needed help. The only reason that Robertson's – total newcomers to yacht sponsorship – decided to support her was that she had once worked there. 'And,' says the commercial director Mike Prest reverently, 'we knew her ...' Clare had clearly made her mark before she ever took to singlehanded voyaging. 'As a determined young woman. Oh yes. Very ambitious, very single-minded.'

In the boardroom they hummed and hawed a little about the risk, as any sponsor must; it was not just the money, but too cosy a household brand-name to contemplate involving in a mid-Atlantic tragedy a thousand miles from nursery teatime. 'Yes, that was at the back of our minds,' admits Mr Prest. 'But we really didn't think any wave would be *impudent* enough to drown Clare.' So the boat got her name, Clare got her backing, and Robertson's got a result which should surely satisfy any sponsor. 'Anybody who wasn't satisfied with that lot', says Mike Prest, 'would have to be a raving mad greedy so-and-so.'

The element of personal faith recurs again and again. The *Financial Times* was persuaded to sponsor the trimaran *FT* by David Palmer, who worked for them; *Old Moore's Almanac* and several other small-scale sponsored boats came into being by the same casual, personal route. Sometimes a major company becomes, a little bemusedly, an incidental sponsor, as with Texaco, the oil company. In 1982 the burgomaster of Nijkerk in Holland wrote to the mayor of Schenectady, N.Y., to present his compliments on 200 years of diplomatic relations between the Dutch and Americans, and to introduce Goos Terschegget, an alderman of Nijkerk wishing 'to remake the passage from the Old World to the New' in the 1984 race – which falls, fortuitously, 300 years after Arendt von Curler of Holland founded the city of Schenectady. This slightly comic-operatic scenario succeeded in including a local Texaco distributor as sponsor for *De Volharding* ('The foolhardy'); and the oil company found itself supporting the boat and disseminating the news. 'It is a small goodwill gesture between ourselves and our distributor', said a representative from head office firmly. 'It is not a

'Kriter VI': sparkling wine travels well

big departure by Texaco into sponsoring boats. No.' But she added, rather wistfully and suddenly no longer an official spokesperson, 'Actually, it all looked such fun at the launching that I rather wish it *was* ours.' Even big companies can be small sponsors.

The real big-time, however, is very big indeed, and not dependent on whims and wistfulness. Experimental fast multihulls in Class I, boats with a real chance of winning, cost hundreds of thousands to build. It is not every singlehander who has the skill and temerity of Alain Colas – who for the 1976 race financed his gigantic *Club Méditerranée* not through direct sponsorship but via a unique entrepreneurial manoeuvre. He told a big newspaper consortium in France that he would feed them news of his project if they would give him free advertising space. He then resold the space to the Club Méditerranée holiday firm for a reported £300,000, got free steel from a steel firm and free electronics from other sponsors. As a result, the finished boat belonged to him personally, and he remained his own master throughout.

That was a rare coup. Most ambitious sailors, having made a reputation in ocean racing, have to present themselves and their project to a sponsor for total support. The French, in a country where yachting stars are more universally fêted than in Britain or America, have taken this to its limits. Paul Ricard's support of Tabarly, the huge infusions of money given by Crédit Agricole and the oil company Elf Aquitaine to Jeantot and Pajot to follow every big race on the international ocean circuit, are proof enough of this. When a new company comes into the sponsorship business in France it does not do so with the cautious 'few thousand' of Cutty Sark or Robertson's; it does it with dash and apparently limitless cash. Take

'Miss Dubonnet': Florence Arthaud, dismasted before the 1980 start, with consoling sponsors on the Plymouth quayside

'Fleury Michon'; France's second largest purveyor of sausages and salamis sponsored the first boat across the 1984 line

Biotherm II, the only Class I boat in the 1984 race to be sailed by a woman. Florence Arthaud is a tough, athletic French sailor; the boat is a 60ft aluminium trimaran; Biotherm itself is a range of skin care preparations based on something known as thermal plankton. Emerging from the marketing department's white-hot crucible, the three elements fuse with fiery French eloquence. 'Florence', says Monique Kern in the Paris office, 'is today's woman. Our woman. *Téméraire, courageuse*, the spirit of *la jeunesse entreprenante*.' The boat is '*haute-technologie, aeronautique*'. The yacht, *comprenez*, represents science and research; Florence represents woman, youth and daring. The sea, presumably, represents plankton. Add it all up and you have a brand image '*parfait*'. There is no anguish, says Mme Kern sternly, about the risk of the voyage. Florence has raced for them before, and overcome bad conditions with courage and flair. The apparent jinx on her OSTAR luck (in 1980 her mast broke on the start line – the boat then was *Miss Dubonnet*, a stroke of bad fortune for the drinks firm) returned in 1984 when both mast and float were damaged on the way to Plymouth, and repaired with only hours to go before the start. 'But', said Mme Kern, 'we have overcome this.' When you have gone so far down the road of identification and publicity, the horrifying cost of shipping a new mast and eight boatbuilding technicians to Plymouth in 24 hours is something which has to be borne; disasters which would put any but the wealthiest private competitor out must not be allowed to spoil an operation on this scale.

Mlle Arthaud, patiently through it all, poses for photographers in glamorous pedal-pushers and wild brown hair. Asked whether she proposes to keep her skin in beauty-parlour condition for the sponsors' image's sake, she is diplomatic. 'You don't have much time; when you have, you sleep. But I, maybe, will take care of myself more than the guys do. Sailors look older than they are, because the sun and the salt and the sea is very bad for skin.' Mme Kern admits that it is 'difficult to maintain oneself *chic* on such a passage'. But Florence will use the creams, she insists, for her own self-image. '*C'est naturel. C'est une femme, quand meme!*'

There is no doubt that the heavily sponsored singlehander carries a unique burden in return for the chance of a winning sail. To be an Arthaud, answering questions on skin care on the eve of a 3,000-mile race, or to be any other sponsored sailor (outside the top few like Tabarly, whose name helps his sponsor rather than the other way round), means being tied to a relentless publicity machine in the very days before the start when the tension is highest. The fatigue of interviews combines with the fatigue of preparation and a sense of debt;

something a sensitive sponsor has to spot and minimize. David Palmer, writing of the stresses he saw on fellow-sponsees, paid tribute to his own paymasters:

> 'The *Financial Times* was generous, helpful and, above all, understanding throughout the project. The pressures that sponsorship put on me were all generated from within myself. Nevertheless, they were there.'

The big sponsors are shy of releasing actual figures spent. '*Pas de chiffres*,' says Mme Kern. Down in the Swansea Centre for Trade and Industry, Swansea City Council representative Mr Burns has no such inhibitions. 'We have spent', he says, drawing breath impressively, 'five thousand pounds.' Misinterpreting my murmur of appreciation, he continued, 'All right, it doesn't sound much, but in times like these it's a lot for us.' Swansea chose to back *Swansea Bay* in 1984 (much as Birmingham City Hall put itself behind *City of Birmingham*) 'to tell

French bank Crédit Agricole backed Jeantot in 1984 but he had ballast problems and capsized

people that we are here, new 600-berth marina, trade opportunities, and all that', and Chris Butler's boatbuilding firm is local. 'The Lord Mayor will send him off with a copy of the city's charter for the mayor of Newport; and we'll post local displays of his progress.' Mr Burns was breezily sanguine on the eve of the race. 'Worries? Are you asking us if we have no confidence in our local boatbuilding industry? He's a hard man. He's going to crash through the waves all the way to Newport.'

So the boats stream out from the dock on a June morning, bearing the names of face creams, of aperitìfs, cities, banks and whiskies; of oil, electronics, scented soaps and motor-cars and biscuits. Perhaps, in some ways, the more distant from seafaring the sponsor's business is, the easier it remains to maintain the vital fantasy. After a mixed

1980 when Daniel Gilard's *Brittany Ferries* came eighth and Bernard Pallard's *Brittany Ferries II* limped home to France early, the most appropriate sponsor of all is taking a break. In the years between 1980 and 1984 the United Kingdom end of Brittany Ferries backed – and got fine value from – the great Chay Blyth in the two-handed Transatlantic and the Round Britain races; but Toby Oliver, for the shipping company, felt, 'We'd had our turn. We're sitting back and looking again at the whole business of sponsorship. As a general view, we reckon that

sponsoring individuals is a dicey way of going about it. We're wary of it.' A reputation for large, safe, landlike boats could be subtly dented, I suggested, by too close an association with small, dicey, tossing ones. 'Yes, quite frankly. Remember that quite a lot of our passengers don't even *like* the sea.' Another sailor may come to convince them over again, as Chay Blyth did; but that ocean crammed with prodigal 'floating ads' is probably as far off now as it was in 1960. There are no certainties in yacht racing; the sea, and the race, will always have cruel

Two views of 'Paul Ricard'. On the left, showing her starboard hydrofoil in 1980, when Pajot raced her as an unofficial entry; bottom, the 1984 version, skippered by Eric Tabarly

jokes to play; not every firm is sporting enough to take them. In 1980, when boats hopefully and expensively named after a bed and a shipping line and a radio and champagne and cigarettes were all disabled by the elements, a boat named after an obsolete sugary drink actually won. But Phil Weld's *Moxie* owed not a penny to the company whose name it bore; Weld, a rich man, had named it that way purely for fun. 'And to express belief in sponsorship. It's a good way for companies to use promotion money.'

*One of OSTAR's more spectacular collisions,
when Tom Grossman's much-fancied 'Kriter VII'
tangled with the Spanish entry 'Garuda' at the
1980 start. Grossman set off again 26½ hours later*

1972

This was the year of the French. And it was the year, as it was bound to be sooner or later, of the multihulls. Catamarans had been tried and found wanting – they were too easily tipped over in rough seas, and would not be really successful until the 1980s and the development of adjustable water-ballast – but trimarans were coming into their own: the French finished first, second, third and fifth, trimarans first, third, fifth and sixth – though there were only six in the race.

A pattern was set, and anyone disposed to doubt how far and how fast the Observer Singlehanded Transatlantic Race had come in a dozen years merely had to compare the record-breaking passage of Alain Colas's trimaran *Pen Duick IV* (the same *Pen Duick* which had come to grief with Tabarly at the helm four years previously) with the leisurely passage of *Jester*. The little junk-rigged folkboat in which Blondie Hasler had come second back in 1960 was now owned and skippered by Michael Richey. He had kept *Jester* up to scratch, and in 1972 he completed the course without mishap. Richey took 58 days to arrive at Newport; Colas had crossed the line more than a month before him. Francis Chichester had to retire – it was to be his last OSTAR.

If British gamesmanship and phlegm had never been in question the single-mindedness of the growing French challenge was breathtaking. Tabarly had inspired a new generation of gritty and highly professional singlehanders; more, he had also set in motion a great swell of national fervour, on whose crest rode excitable sponsors, visionary yacht designers, and some very remarkable, very expensive craft.

Left: Tabarly's 'Pen Duick IV' was sailed by Colas in 1972

Most remarkable (and most expensive) was *Vendredi 13*. She was 128ft long, with a three-masted rig with no mainsails, and was especially designed to race to windward through big seas with a crew of one. She dwarfed every boat around her, her single hull looking something like a modern version of a clipper ship, and she was crewed by Jean-Yves Terlain. In the all-or-nothing world of French dedication to success, coming second is not good enough. Nevertheless, come second she did, just 16 hours behind Colas.

Had the weather been more testing, as it had been in 1968, the 'big boat' might have won. As it was, the incredible success of the multihulls carried conviction. After the fracas of the previous race, when only five out of the 13 multihulled contestants finished, the rules had been tightened up to require not only skippers but also their vessels to have sailed a qualifying 500-mile cruise. If this meant a smaller entry, it also meant that there was only one case of structural failure among the multihulled boats, a cruising catamaran crewed by journalist Murray Sayle. Happily, Sayle was towed into port, and lived to sail another day, as well as to remind us of the troubles and traumas of that year.

In 1972 *The Sunday Times* gamely entered its own catamaran in the race, despite (or possibly because of) the fact that it was sponsored by the rival *Observer*. Sailing *Lady of Fleet* was writer and adventurer Murray Sayle, who claimed no great experience in singlehanded sailing. A fortnight out of Plymouth he filed this report, from a position 39 degrees 34 minutes North, 23 degrees 12 minutes West, approaching the Azores. It is one of the liveliest accounts of solitary voyaging – and shipwreck – to have been inspired by OSTAR.

HUNTING FOR A SEA HOG

Murray Sayle

Night-time is the most intriguing part of the 24 hours. It is now three days since I have seen any kind of ship, apart from a couple of nimble little French and Spanish tuna fishermen earning their livings far from home, and I have to admit that I have begun to relax my vigilance at night somewhat. But with many misgivings.

Sleeping on the saloon floor to be near the cockpit and jumping up every 20 minutes for a look round the dark horizon seems to be getting progressively less profitable, so a couple of nights ago I migrated to the cosy cabin, full of happy memories, set my alarm for two hours, and curled up with a selection of good books. Old habit patterns re-establish themselves quickly.

Lady of Fleet, my Solaris catamaran, was going along easily with a gentle breeze off her beam, the Atlantic chuckling under her hulls, the water lapping in the water tanks, the petrol lapping in the petrol tanks, the Fosters lapping in the cans, and the Scotch lapping in the Glenlivet bottle – a diapason of laps that ought to put anyone to bye-byes.

I tried the early Greek myths. The maiden Epidermis pursued by the fair youth Epiglottis . . . restlessly I turned to Kafka's *The Trial*. Someone must have been telling lies about Joseph K . . . The trouble is I know how that one ends. I returned to what is, these days, my favourite reading: *Reeds Nautical Almanac and Tide Tables* for 1972, a thick blue book, which out here I just can't put down. Apart from being a quarry of hard-won sea lore, Reeds is composed in a unique literary form, half prose, half verse, like some early Norseman's saga.

For a while, I browsed over section XX, Rope and its Uses at Sea.

Worm and parcel with the lay
Turn and serve the other way

is advice which must have comforted many a lonely sailor on a night watch. I turned idly to section XIX, the most riveting read in all of Reeds' 1,240 pages:

Weather Forecasting by single observer. I had just drawn a blanket up to my chin when a couplet leapt from page 5:

At sea with low and falling glass,
Soundly sleeps a careless ass.

In three seconds I was out of my berth and, flashlight in hand, tapping the barometer. It read 1,028 millibars, which is probably a candidate for the *Guinness Book of Records* as one of the highest pressures ever recorded. I tapped the instrument and the needle went up another couple of millibars. Just to be sure, I wound it up, changing the paper, and refilled the ink. The pointer went to 1,032 millibars.

Only when it's high and rising
Truly rests a careful wise one.

I had barely closed my wise eyes when I heard, among the lappings and gurglings, a splash. Not surprising, perhaps, with a thousand miles of sea in every direction. Still . . . I turned to page 805 again. It had to be fate which directed my eye to:

When the sea hog jumps,
Look to your pumps.

I hurriedly consulted the index: Sea Terms, Glossary of, and Sea Creatures, Mythical and Otherwise. No information on what a sea hog might be. To be on the safe side, I went on deck and gazed out into the darkness, featureless except when a wave came creaming into range of my running lights. What am I looking for, I asked myself. A curly tail? Big floppy ears? Still, these old-time sailor men must know a thing or two.

Looking to my pumps, I found that I have, in good working order, two big bilge pumps, two electric bilge pumps, a dinghy pump, a spare hand pump, a spare electric pump and five buckets. I should be able to cope even if the sea hogs start jumping over my mainmast. But I had a look in the bilges just the same. *Lady of Fleet*, being strong and well built, is not making a drip of water in either hull. I tidied up some wood shavings from the

So what does a sea hog actually look like? 'Sunday Times' mariner Murray Sayle searches the briny for creatures of the deep

bilges with a dustpan and brush, checked the compass, checked the wind speed, checked the winches, checked the off-course alarm, had a last look round for the sea hog and returned to a restless bunk, wrestling with:

When the wind shifts against the sun,
Trust it not, for back it will run.

Now let's see. The sun went down in the northwest, while the wind is blowing from west by south, so if it shifted three points, and the sun . . .

I must have dozed off, for when I woke up yesterday there was a fine sparkling morning.

The breeze had died to a zephyr – sea hog was badly out there – and *Lady of Fleet*'s sails hung limp and languid, while the off-course alarm was trilling like a lark.

I made a hearty breakfast of bacon and eggs, with biscuits and marge – 'The wise captain,' says Reeds, 'sees that the crew have plenty of hot, nourishing victuals' – and was just tucking in when I heard, from alarmingly nearby, a honk, or maybe it was a grunt. Anyway a strange noise.

I dashed topside. There, not two cables away (see Nautical Terms, Glossary of) wallowing happily in the swell, all grey and good-natured, was the German ship *Sachsenwald*, her blond crew lining the torpedo deck, her braided skipper, leaning from his bridge, megaphone in hand.

'Excuse, please,' he shouted, 'everythink is all right with you, yes?' I gulped my bacon and egg, found my loud hailer hiding under a pile of Macbean's trawlerman's oilskins, and shouted back: 'Yes, thanks. How about you? Everything OK? Do you know where you are?'

Clouds are gathering thick and fast,
Keep sharp look out for sail and mast . . .

This offer to share my newly gained navigational wisdom was not taken up. My German, I am afraid, is not up to translating.

But I suppose they have their own equivalent, something like '*Wenn Sonne und Englander kommt zusammen, denn kluge Matelots nach dem Hafen gangen*', but while I was working on this, there was a consultation on the bridge of the *Sachsenwald*,

then a smart nautical salute (or were they tilting their foreheads?) and she was away, with a powerful honk of farewell.

I never know how to report these incidents on the daily questionnaire the contestants are filling out for Dr Glin Bennet, the Bristol psychiatrist who is studying how men and women react under the stress of fatigue, fear and loneliness.

When Dr Bennet gave us his sealed packet of questions, with a note that the answers were medically confidential, I suspected we were in for the usual stuff about sex fantasies, masturbation guilt, womb envy, etc.

But Dr Bennet's questions turn out to be very sensible ones, such as would not bring a blush to a Cunard stoker. 'What is your position?' he asks. 'How are you feeling?' 'How much sleep have you had?' And, 'Unusual experiences?' Should I report my failure to sight the sea hog? My obsession with

pump and barometers? Or the fact that my eyes are no sooner closed than I hear a choir of pig-tailed sailormen chanting:

Mackerel sky and mares' tails,
Make lofty ships carry low sails?
What, alone out here, is the usual run of experiences anyway?

I am both relieved and sad to hear that Sir Francis has had to retire. No question of taking over where the old master has had to leave off, of course, but just the same I have checked the emergency supplies. We have 23 Fosters, 15 bottles of Australian Chablis, one Glenlivet, one Haig, one champagne, and one bottle of Corrida red wine, a gift from an enthusiastic colleague.

In all of them, Francis, we drink your health. 39, 28N 21.55W, Midday, Saturday.

I am now picking up the radio beacon on the Island of Santa Maria in the Azores and hope to be

Murray Sayle aboard a still-intact 'Lady of Fleet'

passing through the Azores group towards the end of the weekend. My plan then is to keep on the same course.

'Lady of Fleet' lost her mast in a storm 800 miles east of Bermuda. Sayle radioed this report while under tow from the US coastguards.

Two o'clock on a stormy night is about the worst possible time to be dismasted and, when it happened, it looked as if the Atlantic had calculated the spot farthest from land, sheltered water or help in any shape. Thirteen hours later, however, I was taking a hot shower and an iced grape juice aboard a US coastguard cutter, with *Lady of Fleet* bobbing along behind on a stout towline. Our luck had turned from bad to good almost as fast as the storm which took her mast out.

Inevitably, such things happen when everything seems to be going well. The day of the smash started fine and clear, with a gentle breeze from the south-west and nothing more alarming than a heavy swell from some distant storm.

Such swells, dark-blue hills rolling one after another from the horizon with hardly a patch of white water anywhere, are common in the bit of the Atlantic I was in, and are, in fact, a not unwelcome sign. I was aiming to be just south of the main current of the Gulf Stream, where the warmer water curves back to the south and west to give a small yacht a helping hand of about 20 miles a day.

I planned to follow the edge of the Stream, roughly along the 38th parallel, until I was due south of Halifax in Nova Scotia. From there I reckoned the Gulf Stream and the prevailing south-westerlies should give me a 'downhill' tide to Newport.

Things were going so well that I was beginning to calculate with some certainty that I was ten days away from the finishing line.

Just as well, I thought, because I was getting low on food, and I had run right out of bottled cooking gas. (You can, however, get along on some surprising uncooked meals: raw rice, for instance, is a breakfast you can just about choke down if you grind it with a coffee grinder and soak it for an hour with powdered milk and sugar.) And the petrol, which I needed to generate electricity for navigation lights and the radio telephone, was down to eight gallons. But it looked as if everything would just about last out the voyage.

I had run low on these necessities in my fortnight spent becalmed near the Azores, now 1,000 miles astern. I was now, I thought, in the area where good brisk winds were to be expected. I certainly was.

Luckily, I spent quite a bit of that day on navigation, because I was keen to stay below 39 degrees North. Normally 30 miles or so either way makes no odds in a yacht when you are 1,000 miles from land, but it is well worth the trouble when a few miles too far north would put me into the unfavourable current of the Gulf Stream.

The heavy swell put wrinkles on my horizon and *Lady of Fleet* was looming up and down a lot, so I did five sun-sights at noon and during the afternoon, a shot of the upper edge of the moon when it appeared in daylight, and a sight on the Pole Star, which twinkled through a gap in the clouds at dusk.

The position lines from these shots crossed close to the same spot on the chart – like a bundle of matchsticks arranged by a compulsively neat smoker. Either they were *all* wrong – most unlikely – or I was very close to where I should be.

From dusk I kept a plot every two hours during the night. For someone using only a sextant and chronometer, I was unusually confident of my position.

The barometer, I recorded in my log, started to go down during the afternoon. It was already on the low side – 1,015 millibars – and in an hour it slumped to 1,010. Farther south, the heavy swell, the low glass and the sudden fall would be warning of a possible tropical storm, the disagreeable family which includes hurricanes, cyclones and typhoons. But 38 degrees North is hardly the tropics.

Still, I changed down the headsail twice – lightweather Genoa to No. 1 Genoa and, at 10 pm, No. 2 Genoa, a tall, narrow sail which goes well to windward.

At midnight I was going through a typical small depression of the temperate zone. The wind was averaging 20 knots, falling to 16, when the sky cleared and the moon laid a rocky silver road over the sea, rising to 30 knots as a line of black clouds came over from the south-west. I was carrying the right sail and the night was, in a lonely way, wildly beautiful. But it was time to get some sleep.

I woke just before 2 am. The wind was down to eight knots but the swell was heavier, the blue hills of the afternoon were now black mountains, and a huge black cloud covered the sky. In a minute or two it began to rain, a cloudburst hissing down on the sea. I got into oilskins, deck boots and safety harness and stood in the cockpit puzzling over the instruments which report the wind's speed and direction and the yacht's heading and speed.

Suddenly the rain stopped as if shut off by a tap, the wind speed dropped to 20 knots, and the boat's speed to five. Both speeds hovered for a moment on the dials and then the wind speed needle started to climb fast – to 30, 35, 40. At exactly 40 knots the mainmast crumpled six feet above the deck like a broken match. Mast, Genoa and mainsail went over the side.

All this took perhaps five to ten seconds. As the needle neared 40, I turned, automatically though incredulously, to let the mainsheet go, but I was too late. The boat hardly heeled over at all and the release gear, which lets the headsail go if a capsize threatens, did not operate.

At the same time a heavy sea hit the helpless and stationary yacht and swept over the deck. I heard a bump, which could have been the broken mast hitting the boat's side. Hanging on to the tangle of rigging, I shone a flashlight over the lee side and saw the mast and sails still held fast by the rigging, but sinking under the boat.

If the broken mast was not yet pounding the side, I thought, then it would do when the seas turned the boat round – and any yacht will be holed by this battering ram effect in a few minutes.

I think it was a positive advantage to be alone.

With someone else on board there would have been a discussion about what to do, perhaps an argument about who did it. As it was, I had a simple choice: either to get rid of the broken mast or to somehow stop it holing the yacht, and either course had to be quick. I had no time to be afraid.

I had on board bolt cutters and an axe for just this emergency. It might take 10 minutes to cut loose all the shrouds (fastened by steel wires with an eight-ton breaking strain), with the maximum danger when only one or two still held. But my only real chance of rigging up a temporary sail was to use part of the broken mast or the boom. Then came the argument clincher – my radio aerial had gone over with the mast. And I *had* to rescue that.

In the cockpit I happened to have a long rope – a halyard with a wire rope and a snap shackle on the end of it. I tied a rope to my safety harness to give me a longer leash, kicked off my boots, and with the spare halyard in hand jumped over the side.

The sea, I noticed, seemed absurdly warm, almost tepid, and it blazed with phosphorescence. For the moment the yacht herself sheltered me from the breaking waves.

On the second try I got far enough underwater to get the wire rope snapped round the top of the mast, lying about five feet from the stern. Then I hauled myself clumsily back aboard and got the rope part of the halyard round the powerful main winch in the cockpit and started winching in. It worked. The heavy metal mast began to come alongside, its wad of sail acting as a soft buffer against the hull (I later added a mattress).

I then did the same at the bow, though the winch there had gone overboard with the mast. But I had a powerful block and tackle which my sailor and journalist colleague Nelson Mews had made up for me before the race start – the most useful present I have ever had. With top and bottom secured, the mast was alongside and almost out of the water.

The boat was still pitching wildly and an occasional sea came over the deck and flooded the cockpit, but she rode the seas well and I never had a second's doubt about her stability. I ripped up the floorboard side and, hanging down in the bilge, put my ear to the hull. She was making no water at all and best of all there was no banging or pounding from the mast alongside.

Completing phase one, I went over the side again and, after feeling around in the water, got the aerial back on board. I climbed the surviving mizzen mast and rigged the copper wire into what I hoped was a transmitting position.

It was painful to look forward in a ragged patch of moonlight to where the main mast should have been. *Lady of Fleet* looked like a pretty girl with her front teeth punched in.

After an hour I was trembling and my arms were aching, but I was in a much better position. The yacht was not going to sink and neither was I. I made a quick note in the log: *Object No. 1, save the yacht if I can. But how?*

A quick look at the charts did not offer much hope. Roughly, I put *Lady of Fleet* 660 miles from St John's, Newfoundland, 820 miles from Bermuda, 950 miles from Halifax, Nova Scotia, and 960 from Flores, the nearest of the Azores. Slightly more hopeful, I was 200 miles from the usual station of the American ocean weathership *Echo*. If I could get the propellers back on (I took them off before the start to reduce drag), I had petrol aboard for about 50 miles. It might be possible to cut off the broken mast butt, get the remainder aboard and raise it. But that would be a good week's work for one man.

The yacht would sail after a fashion on only her mizzen and staysail, but she would do two knots – and near the Gulf Stream that might take you to Mexico or Norway or nowhere.

I thought I should give someone ashore my position while I knew it with accuracy. I could hear the British shore station at Portishead on my makeshift aerial, but I could not raise them. Better luck with Ocean Gate, the station outside New York with the intriguing call sign WOO, which heard me on the second try.

I explained to the operator that I was in an interesting predicament but that this was a telephone call and not a Mayday signal.

'I would like to know what ships might be about here', I explained. The operator put me through to the New York headquarters of the US coastguards, which combines the work of Trinity House and the British Lifeboat Service with ice breaking, bridge inspection and other duties in the life-saving sphere. They gave me the radio frequencies of weather ship *Echo*.

'Still afloat but long-term prospect not bright', I noted in the log. 'I can't get a tug to come this far, no merchant ship can afford to slow down to tow me. I am too big to be lifted aboard, which anyway is impossible with this sea running. Best bet: try to get some petrol.'

Little did I guess how near help was. Just 100 miles to my north the coastguard cutter *Chase* was steaming back to America, returning from a training cruise to Britain and Norway with 52 coastguard cadets aboard. She had been to the Azores to refuel – hence her course across a desolate part of the Atlantic seldom used by steamships.

At 3.30 am I was calling up the weathership *Echo* when the duty radio operator on *Chase* replied. They knew all about me and were waiting for instructions. To save my batteries I signed off until daylight and poured myself the last Glenfiddich, when a sudden lurch from *Lady of Fleet* splashed the lot in my face.

For a second or two I wept real tears – reaction from strain, anger, relief, or perhaps just a couple of eyefuls of Scotch and sea water. After that I dozed for an hour or two.

Just after dawn I managed to get through to London by radio after improving the makeshift aerial. The sky had cleared somewhat, but a heavy sea was still running. 'Don't worry,' I was told by *The Sunday Times* office, 'the US coastguard will rendezvous with you at 2.30 this afternoon.'

I can't say I really believed this, but at 2.25 I put my head up for a look. A white ship with a cheerful red, white and blue stripe was bearing down on me, perhaps a mile away. It was the *Chase*.

I forgot my plight for the next few minutes, watching a superb display of seamanship. *Chase* lowered an open motor boat gracefully on to the mountainous seas. The boat came alongside the helpless *Lady of Fleet* – still pitching wildly – and a party of coastguardsmen jumped nimbly aboard. 'We are here to give you a tow', said the chief bosun's mate, a craggy New Englander, as he straightened up the poultice of ropes I had put over the side to keep the mast secure. 'More than a thousand miles?' I asked incredulously. 'Sure,' said the chief. 'That's our job.'

He told me that the skipper of the *Chase*, Captain Bill Aitkenhead, would like a word with me and we went over in the motor boat. Jumping from the ship's boat to a rope ladder lowered down the *Chase*'s side – and later jumping back again – is something I don't want to do too often. Captain Aitkenhead confirmed he was offering me a tow.

'It will have to be where we are going, of course,' he said. 'We are bound for Newport, Rhode Island.'

'I don't want any of your men risking their lives to save my boat', I said. 'It's one of the oldest traditions of the sea', said the captain. 'Besides, it's good training.'

So although I am out of the race, I have high hopes that *Lady of Fleet* will get to Newport just the same. She has stood up magnificently to the ordeal of dismasting and the long tow, and it would have been heartbreaking to have to abandon an undamaged and completely seaworthy yacht just because of a broken mast. And my gratitude goes to the coastguards for their help offered before I could even ask for it. The most I had dared hope for was 200 gallons of petrol.

Consolation also comes from my navigation: I was fewer than seven miles from where I said I was and I have already given a couple of talks to the coastguard cadets on celestial navigation, on the theme that if an amateur like me can learn it anyone can. So perhaps some good may come of all this.

'Jester' has entered every OSTAR since the first. Now the race could barely do without her. Michael Richey, seen here conning the boat from the specially designed midships cockpit, bought her from Blondie Hasler after the 1964 race

No Observer Singlehanded fleet would be complete without an inordinately small, inordinately slow boat called *Jester*. Once upon a time she belonged to the man who dreamed up the whole crazy adventure, Blondie Hasler. Today she is in other, no less dedicated hands, though it is not the kind of dedication that would mean much to those who would rather exclude the little boats from OSTAR altogether. The majority who enter the race still do so as amateur sailors in their own conventional yachts, for their own reasons and at their own expense. *Jester*, which again entered in 1984, is their representative.

JESTER: AN OLD SAILING JOKE

Libby Purves

The big boats come and go; from the classic sloops and ketches of the 1960s to the experimental trimarans and foilers of today, they have brought their varied shapes, their multimasted, computerized, aluminium and carbon-fibre hopes to Millbay Dock over a quarter of a century. Some have failed majestically, for all the cost and skill of their making; some have vindicated it all brilliantly, and whittled the winning time from 40 days to 17. But one little boat has sailed, unchanged, in their impatient wake; and now the race could barely do without her.

Jester has entered every OSTAR since the first. She has given her name to the smallest, most unpretentious class in the race, and become something better than a winner: an institution. She links the futuristic multihulls of the 1980s to the original four little boats which followed Chichester across the Atlantic in 1960. Then, none but *Gipsy Moth* were bigger than her 25 feet; by 1984, 90 of her fellow-starters were bigger, and all were newer boats.

She is as bizarre a sight now as when Lt.-Col. H. G. Hasler entered her for the race he founded in 1960. He called her *Jester* because she was going to be 'such a bloody joke'; the basic wooden folkboat hull – a classic long-keeled small yacht shape – is surmounted oddly by a curving superstructure and a Perspex bubble hatch; instead of the familiar double triangle of a Bermudan rig, she carries a Chinese lugsail, like a little junk, on an unstayed mast. *Jester* is not particularly pretty; not particularly fast (her 1964 record of 37 days was a startling aberration; seven or eight weeks is nearer the mark); and not particularly comfortable. 'Exactly like being in a train in the rush hour,' says one of her rare crewmen, admiringly. Yet *Jester* was fitted by Blondie Hasler, and remains to this day as a supremely simple example of a boat built for one purpose: to take one man, safely and without undue fatigue, out alone into the world's oceans. The junk rig means that the single sail can be reefed or handed from the safety of the cockpit hatch; the strong, long-keeled hull makes for stability and seakindliness; *Jester* is a simple and a faithful boat. On the starting line every four years, her safe record and her homely aspect act as an inspiration and a reassurance to the rest of the fleet; perhaps also as a gentle rebuke to unbridled ambition. When Phil Weld was becoming 'a bit technical' one night before the 1980 race, Michael Richey of *Jester* observed mildly: 'Goodness, Phil, you make me feel like a backwoodsman.' Weld roared with laughter and said, 'Yeah, but we need you, we need you.'

Hasler and 'Jester': she was 'such a bloody joke'

'Jester's tiny tunnel-like interior is not built for comfort any more than the hull is built for speed

'And do you know,' says Richey now, smiling happily into a glass of claret, 'I think he was right. I think they do need us.'

Michael Richey, director of the Institute of Navigation for 33 years, bought *Jester* from Blondie Hasler after the 1964 race; but not with the next OSTAR particularly in mind. He just liked the boat. He enjoyed ocean sailing, and had crewed other boats across the Atlantic; he gains deep satisfaction from navigation itself. In the days of satellite, radar and Decca, he says that transoceanic voyages under sail 'perhaps provide the last opportunity for exercising the art of navigation in its classic form'. Richey has claimed that he only sails for the enjoyment of the navigation; stories circulate about the ship which presumed to drop him a bottle bearing a slip of paper with his position, and of his outrage at this: 'What made him feel his position was more reliable than mine?' After all, navigation, as he once said in a tribute to Chichester, is 'not just a deductive process but a means of self-expression.' So he did not want a fast, hairy, exhausting boat on which to prove himself in arduous foredeck wrestles with giant spinnakers; *Jester* suited him excellently as a boat in which to make voyages. Richey was not really interested in the 1968 OSTAR, only he felt he owed it to the boat to carry on her tradition. Since then, he has been in every race.

The story of Michael Richey's voyages in *Jester* reads like an exposition of his life's philosophy: good-natured, a little austere, profoundly independent in outlook. Behind the handsome, greying, conservative appearance the race accounts reveal a man part monk, part maverick; something, in fact, of a jester himself.

For a start, he decided to use the 1968 race – when the leaders were already aiming at times of 25 and 26 days – as an opportunity to try out one of the old sailing-ship routes across the North Atlantic; the southern route, which extends the distance from 3,000 to 5,000 miles by dipping south and using the trade winds before making up again to Newport. It gives a longer distance, but a better chance, by tradition, of fair winds and currents. He made a contented passage lasting eight and a half weeks, ordering his life with dignity within the cramped tunnel of *Jester*'s interior: he later wrote in the *Journal of the Institute of Navigation*:

'Within the framework of the daily tasks – navigating and sailing the boat, cooking, eating and sleeping – one has somehow to achieve a way of life which satisfies, not by means of distractions but rather by coming to terms with the situation. Being able to live positively under these rather improbable conditions and to enjoy the world is more than half the point. It seems important, for example, to eat well, to prepare the food with care and even to serve it properly; one could be reduced to gnawing in one's bunk.' He eats natural foods: rice, dried meats, and so forth; avoids tins as far as possible, and bakes his own bread. But this is no monastic health-crank:

'As an aid to gracious living I took ten gallons of wine in polythene casks. The living must have been too gracious for it only lasted half-way.'

In what he called this 'almost interplanetary isolation' he voyaged to Newport, and arrived unnoticed and unheralded, a full week after the last finisher. There he found to his horror that – carrying no radio – he had been 'in danger of being forcibly rescued' from his comfortable existence.

Richey is not competitive. 'The point', he explained to me years after this voyage, over lunch, 'is that I do *not* care who is ahead or behind. But I *do* care about doing it well or badly; making that voyage, making decisions, is like making anything else well or badly – a poem, or a picture, or a table, or a sculpture' (he was once a sculpture pupil of Eric Gill). 'I go on the race to make a voyage as well as it can possibly be made, in *Jester*.' Then why, one wonders, pursue this almost Zen approach in the context of an ocean race? 'Actually, I do it for the company. There is a sort of social organism; individuals together on one ocean; it is consoling.' And, he adds with a slight return of austerity, it does provide a motive. 'I am a great believer in the danger of motiveless sailing. If you get to the point where it doesn't matter whether you go downwind or across the wind, you might as well be on a li-lo.' He is, after all, a former naval officer.

However, after another race in 1972, when he took just as long and came second last, in 1976 he did not complete the voyage at all. Five or six hundred miles west of Fastnet, out in the ocean, Richey thought: 'Oh, the hell with this', and decided to cruise the south-west coast of Ireland instead.

Typically and tranquilly, there seems to have been no frustration or self-reproach about this. 'I quite wanted to do that cruise, to see someone who was living there; so I replaced one aim with another.' He sailed into Cork, and sent a polite and honest telegram to the Royal Western:

JESTER RETIRED IN FAVOUR OF AN IRISH CRUISE
STOP NO DAMAGE OR PROBLEMS

And yet, in 1980, when they did have damage and problems of a frightening sort, Richey and *Jester* went on to finish. 'Oh, the stupidest thing happened . . . a small fixture on the yardarm, stainless steel, but it broke. A terrible twist-up.' He was two days out, and 60 miles west-south-west of Fastnet, when the entire rig collapsed, leaving him no way of raising the sail on its yard. He managed to hoist two

panels of the Chinese sail, and in this crippled and unmanoeuvrable fashion limped homeward at $1\frac{1}{2}$ knots. *Jester* having no engine, he could make no progress except downwind.

Now, if you are a competitive spirit in a highly-bred boat – as was, for example, Florence Arthaud in the same race – and you are dismasted on the starting line, you don't even consider carrying on. No hope of winning means no point in doing the race at all; you retire sadly and immediately. What do you do, though, if you are an uncompetitive spirit, dedicated only to the 'making of good voyages'? In this case, the answer is that you limp into Plymouth, have dinner with your friend the boatbuilder Alec Blagdon, catch the night train to London and thence down to Brighton to collect the boat's original yardarm from a loft, and take it back for refitting.

The journey across London by Underground, says Richey, was 'a strange interlude in a race, like the dream sequence of a film'. On 18 June, 11 days after the starting gun (Phil Weld was only six days away from Newport) *Jester* set out again into the Atlantic. There was such 'a conspicuous lack of urgency' that Richey actually stopped for the night off the seaside village of Cawsand rather than brave a foggy start. He quoted in his log Admiral Troup's 'outward bound, don't run aground', and spent 'a peaceful night at anchor'.

At last, 69 days after the original start and 47 after her restart, *Jester* arrived in the New World with more memories to add to her days at sea. In 'The Troublesome Voyage', his modest account in the *Royal Cruising Club Journal*, Richey wrote of compensations mental and physical for his doggedness: lunches of white cabbage with garlic and oil, pleasant days running one into the other in the sun, 'a curiously named French saucisson called Jesus de Lyon'. He also, as in all his brief accounts of ocean voyaging, describes the unhappiness, the need for total self-containment in times of lethargy and dejection; calms when 'every day starts with the same heavy feeling, the same silence'. Reading Richey's logs gives one of the most honest pictures we have of a man's mind on such a voyage; 60 days after the first hopeful start, with the 'social organism' of fellow-contestants all dispersed and gone from the face of the sea, *Jester* was very much alone:

'I had been set further north than I intended, and seemed shackled to the spot. I had run out of literature and my food supplies were dwindling. My nerves too seemed to be a bit frayed, one day the bean stew landing up in the bilges, on another the spaghetti in my bunk. My sense of well-being seemed at its nadir.'

In such times he quotes Conrad: 'To surrender all personal feeling in the service of that fine art is the

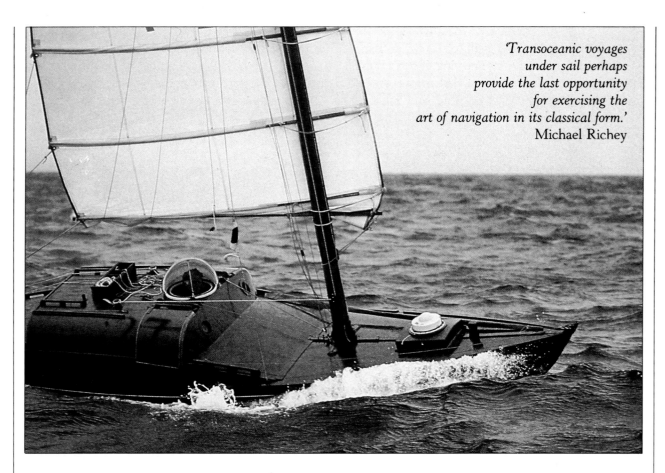

'Transoceanic voyages
under sail perhaps
provide the last opportunity
for exercising the
art of navigation in its classical form.'
Michael Richey

only way for a seaman to the faithful discharge of his trust.' There is little joy, he says, in the 'merely pleasurable' at sea.

1984 may be *Jester*'s last OSTAR; not because in 1988 her master will be 72 years old and she 35, but because, now retired, Richey 'would like to sail her around the world'. Both are in good enough shape to do it; the skipper is free enough, and tough enough, after a sociable but bachelor life, to take off for a time alone; the boat has just had a £10,000 refit. This was paid for in an entirely typical way: certainly not by any sponsor, nor by the sort of whimsical personal wealth that spends more on an old boat than she would be worth in the saleyard. Richey had to raise the wind; and so, from his flat in Brighton, he had a London auctioneer offer for sale a rare collection of treasures: drawings, engravings, books and personal autograph letters from his late sculpture-master Eric Gill and his lifelong friend the artist David Jones. 'I managed to reach the figure and keep a few things back. One or two of them I minded losing; well, I minded who bought them really. Dealers . . . But,' he continues happily, 'being without issue, one does wonder why one has all these things anyway.' So fragments of past life paid for *Jester*'s future voyages; and in any case, the pleasures of memory and imagination, aesthetics and orderliness, flow as freely to Michael Richey from his voyages as from any art collection. In the midst of what he called the 'troublesome voyage' of 1980, he describes a spell of fine southerly weather,

making progress after a long, depressing calm:

'Typically, I would rise at eight, read the log and take my first sight, eat breakfast (bacon or muesli, tea or coffee) and then work the sight up. Ablutions comprised a bucket bath on the foredeck, the safety harness made fast around the mast. Then, in the sun, sitting with my feet in the control hatch, I would read; perhaps St Paul for a while, and then whatever larger work I was engaged in (after Gibbon it was the *Mabinogion* and then the works of Henry Green). In those latitudes a sight around noon made sense and when the position had been recorded in the log, the day's run computed and so on, lunch, an alfresco affair with wine. I would read the afternoon away, pleasurably in the sun, and in the evening mix a drink (wine, water and lemon juice). Perhaps another sight and then the evening meal, generally spaghetti. Afterwards I might get something on the radio or play music on the tape recorder; the light below was not bright enough to read. But I enjoyed the snugness of the saloon, lit with a soft glow. And so, for a while at least, to bed.'

Looking at *Jester* in harbour – a tiny tunnel-like interior, barely a flat piece of deck to sit on – such Olympian contentment is hard to envisage. But her master sails her on; soon, perhaps, beyond the Americas and towards Pacific horizons. Well-made voyages make him happy; bounded in his nutshell, a king of infinite space.

1976

The 1976 race began in the glare of controversy and finished in the shadow of a double tragedy: the loss at sea of two yachtsmen whose deaths remain a matter of conjecture. Mike Flanagan's *Galloping Gael* was found drifting in mid-Atlantic without her skipper aboard; Mike McMullen and his trimaran *Three Cheers* vanished altogether.

Ironically, neither sailor was a victim of the dangers that had caused such heated arguments at the start of the race – the dangers presented by the huge size and untried technical innovations of some of the boats. McMullen himself had drawn attention to them. 'I think I have a very good chance', he had said before the race. 'A lot of the large yachts, and particularly the big multihulls, are simply not suitable for singlehanded sailing.'

The editor of *Yachting World* was even more outspoken, arguing that *The Observer* should be ashamed for letting the dimensions of the race get out of hand, and accusing the Royal Western Yacht Club of naiveté and megalomania. The focus and inspiration of such talk, pointedly ignored by the singlehanded fraternity, was the monstrous 236ft four-master entered by Alain Colas. *Club Méditerranée* was, Christopher Brasher pointed out, longer than an Icelandic gunboat ... 'but unlike an Icelandic gunboat, it has only one man aboard.' The fact that her huge hull was packed with the latest electronic navigation equipment failed to silence the Cassandras. They saw Colas's clipper-sized vessel being a danger to himself and other shipping. There were other big boats besides, including a renamed *Vendredi 13*, two multihulls over 60ft and Tabarly's 73ft ketch *Pen Duick VI*.

Neither *Galloping Gael* nor *Three Cheers*, however, were in this category. It must be assumed that what caused their skippers' deaths was quite simply the weather. Some competitors counted seven gales during the crossing; several encountered storm-force winds, as well as treacherous fogs and calms. There were dozens of sinkings and gear failures and, certainly, some of the more sophisticated craft proved unequal to the conditions. Jean-Yves Terlain's 70ft catamaran *Kriter III* broke up in heavy seas; *Club Méditerranée* had to put in to Newfoundland for repairs; Yvon Fauconnier was injured aboard the second largest boat in the race, *ITT Oceanic* (formerly *Vendredi 13*).

Traditionalists were pleased that it was a monohull (though a large one), Tabarly's big black *Pen Duick*, that came through the gales to be first across the line. Other, more modestly-sized monos did well, including Clare Francis's *Robertson's Golly* (breaking the women's record) and the little 24ft Czech entry *Nike*, smallest boat to survive the ordeal of 1976. But for multihullers there was also a triumph when the 31ft trimaran *The Third Turtle* scooted smartly across the line to take third place less than a day behind *Club Méditerranée*. So even the worst that Atlantic depressions could do to the singlehanders had not resolved the great mono/multi debate. What it had done, though, was to place a sizeable query beside the notion that bigger is necessarily better, or newest necessarily fastest.

Above: 'Galway Blazer'. Left: Clare Francis

Alain Colas was one of the hardest of the hard men from France. He won the Observer Singlehanded Race in 1972 in *Pen Duick IV*. Four years later he came second. But it was not his speed that inspired admiration so much as the craft in which he achieved it. *Club Méditerranée* is the biggest boat built to be raced singlehanded. *Observer* columnist Michael Davie went to Millbay Dock before the 1976 race to examine the phenomenon.

A MAN AND HIS MONSTER
Michael Davie

The evening was fine, the smell of oil agreeable: the moon shone in a clear sky. I walked through the first of the three dock harbours, noting, with respect but without surprise, a group of experienced-looking but orthodox boats tied up alongside one another. No one was about. Then I rounded the corner of a warehouse into the next dock and felt a shock of pure amazement.

From reading my own newspaper, I had gathered that the favourite for the race was a very large French boat. I had seen photographs of it. They had left me totally unprepared. Photographs, by and large, do not convey scale. Even the information that this particular boat can carry 40 people had not greatly impressed me; so can a London bus.

How can one get the point across? The boat has been specially designed – this is the first point to bear in mind, to grasp the nature of the phenomenon – to be driven by one man. Given this condition, it is colossal, gargantuan, absurd.

It is 236ft long and 36ft wide. It is three times the size of the *Golden Hind*, the ship in which Drake circumnavigated the globe. It is five times as big as the famous *Gipsy Moth IV* that Sir Francis Chichester sailed round the world. Its length is six times the height of an ordinary two-storey house (usually 40ft from the ground to the top of the roof); and 40 times the height of the man who sails it.

To the layman and indeed to many serious sailors, it seems barely conceivable that one man can handle such a monster. Yet it has already been done. The man in question, Alain Colas, aged 32, has already sailed the thing – named, for reasons that will shortly appear, the *Club Méditerranée* – on one singlehanded trip of 1,500 miles. (The Atlantic is 3,000 miles across.)

I walked up and down the jetty, examining the brute, painted dark blue, with four towering masts. The deckhouse looked as big as a decent-sized sitting-room. From it, a man emerged whom I recognized as Colas and leaned on the guard rail.

He looked, in the dusk, unnervingly like the briefly celebrated Ronald Milhench: narrow-faced, extravagantly bushy mutton-chop whiskers. He wore a dark sweater. I had already decided that the man who proposed to sail such an extraordinary artefact across the Atlantic must be in the grip of an idea. If he was engaged in a search for pleasure, or privacy, or himself, he could have chosen – like other competitors – a more normal craft.

Colas won the last of these transatlantic races, four years ago. But in an orthodox-sized boat. Only vision could explain the switch. I asked him, therefore, whether he believed there was any theoretical limit to the size of boat that a man could sail singlehanded. He appeared to give the question thought, and peered off into the distance.

'*Je ne sais pas*,' he said finally. '*Je ne crois pas.*'

He paused again and said with solemnity, 'One day, we shall know.'

We talked for a few minutes more, but he seemed tense and even uneasy. When he went back into the deckhouse he walked with a bad limp.

Next morning I learned the story of the limp, and of how and why Colas comes to be driving, even now, this huge machine across the Atlantic. He hails from the middle of France, where his father has a small pottery factory, employing some ten men, near Nevers. Colas became a teacher, and, being of restless disposition, ten years ago found himself teaching French in Sydney, Australia.

Twelve years ago, the transatlantic race was won by a French naval officer, Eric Tabarly, who became a French national hero, on the lines of Francis Chichester in Britain. Tabarly passed through Sydney, and Colas attached himself to him as crew. He became Tabarly's protégé. Sailing through the Pacific, he scooped up a Tahitian wife.

But although Colas won the race four years ago, what excited his imagination was the performance of the second boat, also French: a boat regarded as perhaps too big for one man to handle, *Vendredi 13*. It was not; and Colas decided that *Vendredi* had proved that the way to get speed was sheer size. He therefore conceived the notion of a boat twice the size of *Vendredi*.

It is not clear whether, at that stage, he was thinking only about racing. It is clear now that racing forms only a small part of what he is up to. His idea is that the sailing ship, transformed by modern technology, is ready for a comeback.

Colas expects to cross the Atlantic in 18 days. If he does, he will have demonstrated that his boat

Alain Colas and 'Club Méditerranée' came second in the 1976 race

really works. He will then attempt to propagate the idea that such boats, with a very small crew, can be ecologically appropriate (no oil) cargo boats of the future. Given the current price of ship and air freight, there may be something in the idea. There is certainly plenty of cargo space inside the Colas boat; it is like a London Underground station.

He had the idea of a giant boat; the next problem was to raise the money to build it. His victory had given him the exaggerated status that the French often attach to their sporting heroes, who, like other inappropriate national symbols, such as Concorde, are somehow felt to have added to *la Gloire*. He conceived a brilliant scheme.

He told a consortium of some 50 French provincial newspapers, with a combined daily circulation of seven million copies, that he would feed them news of his next project if each paper would donate to him, free, some advertising space. He was supported by Gaston Defferre, the long-time mayor of Marseilles, who ran for the presidency against de Gaulle and is the main newspaper owner in Marseilles. The consortium agreed.

Colas then sold the advertising space to the Club Méditerranée for £300,000. He secured free steel from a steel firm, and free electronic equipment from sponsors. The monster was built.

One of the leading French yachting writers, M. Jean-Michel Barrault, of *Voiles et Voiliers*, told me he thought that the value of *Club Méditerranée*, today, given its fame throughout France, might not be far short of a million pounds. It belongs, outright, to Alain Colas.

Amateur yachting has boomed and is booming in France: French sponsors are more serious about the transatlantic race than British sponsors, and the big money concentrated in *Club Méditerranée*

symbolizes the way that sponsorship may distort – instead of supporting – the notion of amateur ocean racing.

Colas was helped prepare for sea last week by 15 young students from the merchant navy training school at Le Havre. The other competitors, including some of the French competitors, deal in understatement, modesty, the low profile. Colas arrived and called a press conference, a thing no other competitor would dream of doing. He protested passionately because the committee that organizes the race banned his satellite-assisted navigation system, as not being in the spirit of the race. He showed his displeasure by refusing to emerge from his boat for 24 hours.

His ill-humour, though, may have had to do with more serious misgivings than his claim that he has been singled out for unfair treatment by the organizers. One experienced yachting observer said last week that Colas seemed 'frightened' of his boat. Anyone else would be. The thought of being alone in her during a Force 9 gale is unimaginable. And there is the limp.

A year ago, Colas was anchoring in a port in Brittany when a nylon rope, attached to the anchor chain, caught round his right leg. It stripped the bone – so that his foot was attached to his leg only by bare bone and the achilles tendon. Almost anyone else would have passed out. Colas managed to cut the rope with a knife, and to get his hand to the pressure point. He held the foot on to his leg, in case, as he said later, the surgeons needed it. He was in hospital for six months. Almost anyone else would have abandoned all idea of any race. Colas had his hospital room papered with plans of the boat and continued his preparations, adjusting the gear to his crippled state.

Four months ago, his leg in plaster, he held court at the Paris Boat Show with a special stand to himself, a model of his boat and a large sign saying '*Le Grand Bateau*'.

The plaster is now off, but he wears a surgical boot. He admits that he is in pain. He is thus under pressure from the size of his boat, from his sponsors, and from his foot. He has been deprived of the foolproof navigation equipment that he relied on during his proving voyages.

Colas told me that he is a Catholic. He talks in a mystical fashion about man getting to know the wind and sea better, partly, it appears, through improved instruments and partly through finer tuning of his God-given senses. If Colas gets favourable weather, he may sail across with spectacular ease. If he does not, he may find himself engaged in a bizarre and most demanding battle on two fronts, both with the Atlantic and with his monstrous vehicle.

Alain Colas crossed the line in second place, having lost valuable time putting into Newfoundland for repairs. This is his account of that memorable, gale-ridden race. Tragically, it was the last OSTAR in which he competed. He was lost at sea two years later, racing in the Route du Rhum.

THE SKIPPER'S STORY

Alain Colas

I know now that it is possible to win the Observer Singlehanded Transatlantic Race in 18 days with *Club Méditerranée*, although my time of 24 days and three hours in this year's race, a few hours behind the winner, Eric Tabarly, suggests otherwise.

The bald record doesn't tell about the four days that my 236ft, four-master stretched her legs and reeled off exhilarating 24-hour runs of over 200 miles on the wind. Nor does it tell about the halyard failures that plagued this powerful, seaworthy ship. It doesn't tell of the several other days we came close to 200-mile runs.

The record won't show either that I completed the first half of the crossing in a mere eight days. In short, it won't show the great potential for safe, comfortable speed under sail that exists in my big sailing ship.

Despite all the setbacks it has still been a happy passage for me because I was so glad to be back at sea on both my legs and I was so glad that *Club Méditerranée* was proving herself powerful and seaworthy, that she could take the rough going and that I could be full master of her at all times.

I should explain a little about all the various systems that were designed to make it possible for one man efficiently to race such a large vessel. The key control is a Wang 2200 desk-top computer which monitors all the activity and all the instrumentations aboard the boat. Special programmes

Left: The enormous 'Club Méditerranée' in which Colas crossed the Atlantic in just over 24 days

developed by the Compagnie International de Services Informatique do everything from reducing sextant sights and automatically decoding broadcast Morse-code weather information to monitoring for bilge water or the presence of hydrogen from overcharging batteries.

A video display screen on the computer shows me instant readings from 14 different instrumentation points. An alarm sounds the moment any of these readings drops below or goes above predetermined levels. There are the obvious ones such as boat speed, wind direction, and wind speed, or the subtle touches such as the humidity alarm which warns me about dropping humidity which in turn signals a break in the fog which permits me to snatch a sight. The computer also monitors the ship's diesel generators as well as the solar, wind and water generators and their charging rates.

There is other sophisticated equipment on board that the race committee refused to let me use – a satellite navigation system driven by another computer that prints my position every eight minutes, a facsimile receiver that prints weather maps and other data charts transmitted by radio signal and, of course, my radar. I knew the committee would not relent on the radar or the facsimile receiver, but I was extremely sad when they published a special rule a few days before the start, banning my satellite navigation system.

At the start in Plymouth Sound I was ready for action and determined not to let any of this spoil my race. I knew my boat well and I was determined to get a dinghy start which I did, right on the gun in company with the US sailor Mike Kane in his *Spirit of America*.

Dawn on the second morning of the race found me tacking in light air in company with other boats off the Scilly Isles at the entrance to the English Channel. As the breeze filled in, I worked away from Jean-Yves Terlain on the big catamaran *Kriter*, with whom I'd been exchanging tacks. By late afternoon I was passing the old *Vendredi 13*, now named *ITT Oceanic*. This was a good omen.

During that night I passed a large ketch. It had to be my rival, Eric Tabarly aboard *Pen Duick VI*, which had been sailing away from us all very smartly and briskly at the start of the race.

Now I could have my first sleep. I was clear of land, of the shipping lanes and, as far as I could guess, of all my competition. That night I slept for short periods of two and three hours at a time. The breeze filled in from the SSE and *Club Méditerranée* began to march along at a steady 10 knots.

It was foggy again, heralding what was to be the start of a very foggy passage. Altogether there were 14 days of fog during my 24-day crossing.

The boat was still logging 10 knots the next day

as the wind built to 35 knots. I was carrying all sail except the No. 3 staysail because its wire headstay chafed against the radar superstructure every time the wind got over 30 knots.

Under those conditions the boat just eased along smoothly, with dry decks and with a 12-degree angle of heel. She has fine ends and long straight runs and is very easily driven.

On 9 June the wind came ahead and as I beat into heavy seas I had the first of a series of recurrent problems with halyards. Twice the halyard for the No. 1 staysail broke and each time it was several hours' work to retrieve the sail and set it again. It was wet work, but not too wet: the bow of the boat is 15 feet off the water.

It was a very tired skipper who dragged himself into bed that night after wrestling with the jib. I could barely walk.

The halyard problem was to plague me throughout the voyage and would eventually force me to put into St John's in Newfoundland. The halyards were 10 mm thick and there were five reeved off and ready for use on each mast but they were just not strong enough to take the strain as the boat pounded into head seas. They would break at the sheave.

It's not my custom to break gear. You simply can't afford the heavy cost in time and effort of broken gear on a big boat. But remember that I built the boat by telephone from my hospital bed and that this was the only problem in a very worthwhile project.

At noon on 11 June, with the race six days old, I had completed more than one-third of the distance from Newport even though I twice more had had problems with broken halyards.

Although it only takes me about 10 minutes to hoist a sail on *Club Méditerranée* and another 10 minutes to sheet it in and adjust the traveller to my satisfaction, the work of clearing the broken halyard and getting the sail ready to hoist again usually involved several hours of extremely hard work.

By nightfall it was blowing a gale again. It blew

Mike Kane's 'Spirit of America', which didn't finish

'Vendredi 13' renamed 'ITT Oceanic' in 1976

steadily for several hours during the night at 45 knots and *Club Méditerranée* snored on strongly on port tack. I had already doused staysail No. 4 but the blow cost me a No. 1 staysail. The masthead block for the third halyard let go and the sail went overboard and that was the end of it. I got it back on board with a lot of work but I did not have the facilities to repair it. From that time on, I had to crank in some weather helm on the automatic pilot to balance the boat.

During the night and the morning I had to douse several sails because the boat was crashing into seas that were building to about 20 feet in height. Nevertheless, my noon position on 12 June showed that *Club Méditerranée* had made a good 176 miles to windward during the gale.

As the weather eased in the afternoon I had to hoist two staysails and one mainsail and it proved to be an exhausting battle. Each sail is 1,200 square feet and has full-length wooden/plastic composite battens. I estimate that each sail with battens weighs about 400 pounds, so it isn't easy. But I had chosen to do it.

There was a day's respite with light easterlies before the glass started falling quickly again. For a while the wind came out of the south at 30 knots and the boat was smashing its way through big seas on a close reach at 18 knots. Then the glass really dived and the wind came ahead. I lowered staysail No. 4 while staysail No. 2 obligingly lowered itself when the halyard broke. It wasn't too hard to get the sails under control. The battens helped and there were also jiffy-reefing lines and a headboard downhaul to help muzzle the sail.

By the evening of the eighth day I had passed the half-way mark in the race. It was a heavy, hectic night again with 50 knots of wind at dawn and now I was in for a real storm with the wind settling at 50 knots and the seas running around 25 feet.

Soon I was reduced to carrying only Nos. 1, 2 and 3 mainsails, which I tried to feather along on their

Tabarly's big racing ketch 'Pen Duick VI', winner of the 1976 OSTAR. *Overleaf: 'Club Méditerranée'*

travellers. It blew at 50 knots for two days before the glass started to rise and I began to anticipate a following easterly breeze, having worked north of the low. But the low shot north and caught me again and now I was in for a 60-knot westerly storm with vicious seas.

Before I could douse mainsail No. 1 it was ripped off the mast and it was a long fight to subdue it. During this time mainsail No. 2 came to mischief although I managed to get down mainsail No. 3 without damage.

I was under bare poles for several hours while line squalls came whistling through with gusts of up to 70 knots. The boat started shipping seas on deck around this time with several crests going above the pilot house.

Even sails that had been properly furled and tied down suffered chafe problems in these conditions, and although the storm moderated on 15 June, it took me all day working without a break to do sufficient repairs to have two staysails and two mainsails hoisted by 8 pm. I could hardly walk. I had to crawl to my bunk with sore, aching hands. It was real exhaustion, but the boat was sailing.

The following day the wind dropped away entirely and I spent the whole day sewing sails. For two days I worked to repair mainsail No. 2 because I didn't have sufficient sail area forward and, although my speed was good, the boat's manoeuvrability was impaired.

The turning point in the race came at 2 am on Friday, 18 June, when the second halyard on staysail No. 2 let go, leaving me with only one halyard available for the only sail I could use on the forward half of the boat. I hoisted it again with the third and last halyard, but I was getting worried.

Club Méditerranée was approaching the fishing grounds and the shipping lanes and it was not very seamanlike to continue in the fog at good speed without the ability to tack quickly or to change course. I decided that because St John's was on my way, I would stop and reeve off new halyards and attempt to repair sails. I knew that my No. 1 mainsail was beyond repair so I used the radio-telephone to call home to tell my brother to bring some more halyards and the mainsail.

With the enthusiastic help of many people in St John's we repaired sails and rove off new halyards, all the time believing a French radio report that Tabarly had been sighted off Cape Race, ahead of me. Now that I've seen his chart I estimate that I had a 330-mile lead when I put into St John's.

In the last week as I sailed towards Newport my hopes rose again as days went by and there was still no word of Tabarly's finishing. However, my hopes were dashed in the early morning hours of 29 June when I heard coastguard radio traffic about Tabarly's arrival, only seven hours before I finished.

Now I must find fresh tasks for my big ship. It is possible she could become a charter vessel, but I'd prefer to undertake work of some kind in the field of scientific research. With her ability to do fast, comfortable passages under sail and to produce one kilowatt a day of free electricity through the sun, sea, and wind, *Club Méditerranée* could make proving voyages for commercial wind-ship routes, or perhaps undertake oceanographic research work requiring an absence of engine noise.

And, of course, there is always the next single-handed race, four years from now.

Tom Grossman in 'Kriter VII' in 1980; he came tenth, despite losing 26½ hours at the start after colliding with 'Garuda'. Right: Desmond Hampton of Britain, in 'Wild Rival'

1980

If traditional hulls had come back into the reckoning with Tabarly's victory in 1976, the first six boats across the line four years later seemed to indicate that the tide had turned decisively in favour of the multihull fraternity. One of these yachts, the futuristic foiler *Paul Ricard*, was not in fact an official entry: Eric Tabarly had been forced to scratch at the last minute because of an old skiing injury and Marc Pajot, who had taken over in his place, had not had time to do the qualifying cruise before the start. Nevertheless, *Paul Ricard*'s performance could not be ignored when it came to assessing the overall impact of the 1980 results: Phil Weld's *Moxie* had not only set a new record, but she was followed home by five other trimarans, each of which had also smashed the old record set by Colas in 1972, Pajot coming in an unofficial fifth.

But one had to be circumspect about drawing the obvious conclusions: the weather had been a lot kinder and the winds a lot more helpful than in 1976. The old doubts about the ruggedness of multihull yachts when high speeds confronted foul weather or whales or floating wreckage could not yet be tossed overboard. Mike Birch's *Olympus Photo* lost a sizeable lump from her bridge deck as a result of the waves' continuous pounding. Though she managed to come through in fourth place, the accident was a clear warning to multihull designers of the stresses such craft have to endure.

No such anxieties marred the scene in Newport as the finishers followed each other in, however. The weather and the record-breaking times aside, the best reason for celebration was that the winner was not only the oldest sailor in the race but also the first American ever to have won. Another was the fact that the first husband and wife rivalry came to a happy conclusion, with both Rob James and his wife Naomi completing the course in good times.

For the organizers, the results were another kind of triumph: they had proved that the new restrictions on the length of yachts (56ft) and on the size of the entry (110 boats) had in no way marred the quality of the event. There had been a great deal of grousing when the revised rules had been unveiled, especially from the French. But the Royal Western had won wide public support when the race committee chairman, the venerable Jack Odling-Smee, had announced the decision: 'We have amended the rules for three reasons. First, we do not want to be a menace to other shipping in the Channel. Second, we want to make sure that more yachts actually reach the other end of the course, and third, we have set class limits to try to adhere to the original concept of the race – which is to defeat the ocean rather than the other competitors.'

This was also the first race in which Argos transponders, beaming up to communications satellites orbiting over the Atlantic, had been fitted to every yacht in an attempt to keep track of the race as it unfolded. The system was not altogether successful and nearly one-third of the fleet was 'lost' when damp seeped into the transponder casings. But at least the principle of satellite surveillance was firmly established as an element in the race, with benefits both for safety and press coverage. And as luck would have it, one yacht whose transponder was not put out of action by salt and spray was Phil Weld's. *Moxie* was homed in on, all the way home.

Left: Nick Keig's 'Three Legs of Mann III' came in second place in 1980

Top and above: Rob and Naomi James, first husband and wife contestants, both did well in 1980. Rob was later drowned off Salcombe when the netting on his trimaran, 'Colt Cars', gave way

Top, above and right: Chris Butler on board his Achilles yacht. In 1980 he was 41st in 'Achillea' and in 1984 the renamed 'Swansea Bay' took him to 45th overall and first in Class V

Phil Weld, the veteran American yachtsman, won the 1980 Observer/Europe 1 Singlehanded Transatlantic Race in a dazzling record time. When his trimaran *Moxie* breezed across the finishing line at Newport, Rhode Island, those who didn't know him registered some surprise: he was, after all, the oldest man in the race. Not Phil Weld, however. Nearly a year before the race he had penned this prediction for Boston's *Sail* magazine.

WHO'S GOING TO WIN?
Phil Weld

My hunch is that the 1980 winner will reach Brenton Reef in less than 18 days. The early qualification deadline will result in a fleet that's had nine months to test rigs and gear. Among the boats assembled in Millbay Dock for scrutineering on Monday, 2 June, there should be little of the last-minute scrambling to fit out that has prevailed before. Among the fans, some will deplore the trend away from Hasler's tiny, junk-rigged *Jester* and the 1960 classic *Gipsy Moth*. But this time, to be considered a serious contender, a boat ought to have sailed 300 miles in 24 hours, or at least have proved able to do so, and proved she can average seven knots 'made good' on the wind in moderate air for several consecutive days. Ever more rapid crossings are implicit in the definition of the 'object of the race':

'The race is intended to be a sporting event, and to encourage the development of suitable boats, gear and technique for singlehanded ocean crossings under sail.'

The evolution of the easiest passagemaker for the solo sailor seems to be leaning toward the medium-sized, light-as-possible trimaran. She can maintain high average speeds with relatively small sail area and correspondingly light gear, a combination helpful in reducing skipper fatigue. The same could be said of catamarans.

So let's see what else the favourites will have in common, besides boat type. They should all have raced in at least one OSTAR or its equivalent. One man alone should be able to tack or gybe the boat in under a minute, reef the main in less than five. Sails, cleats, blocks, halyards, pad-eyes – all will have been gale-tested.

A skipper who can't say: 'I have no boat worries' doesn't belong on the bookies' list. But what of his other worries? Let's consider some of the matters that have been causing contestants to concentrate during the pre-race months.

Fitness – Learning to get along on no more than five hours' sleep in 24 represents a training goal that comes easier the older you are. Catnaps to the sleep-starved become like sips of water to the raft survivor. An hour's deep sleep to the lone voyager can carry him or her through 12 critical hours at the helm. At both the start and finish, the threat of collision requires wakefulness punctuated by snatches of sleep only while lying in the cockpit.

Apart from sleep control, the physical training for the race demands about the same sort of toughening as any endurance contest. Shorthanded, or better still two-handed, ocean racing – preferably with someone not so strong nor so experienced – seems the best preparation.

Toughening palms to handle lines without wincing takes two to three weeks. So the competitors shouldn't leave them soft until Plymouth.

The readiness to change sail – up or down – will separate the pros from the amateurs toward the end of the race when light airs will prevail. Going up from small reacher to big may require exertion every bit as strenuous as a set of singles.

For these stresses one must have nourished the will to win – an attitude that comes naturally to most serious international athletes, but not necessarily to solo sailors, who are often philosophic types quite simply rewarded by having made a fast passage against odds. It's impossible to engender the killer instinct against one's friends, all of whom are, like yourself, contending against the true adversary – the wind, or the lack of it.

Like infantrymen in opposing fox-holes, opponents share bonds of commonly experienced discomfort and frustration that make adrenalin-pumping hatreds difficult to summon. And yet the ambitious skipper must somehow sharpen his appetite for victory if he hopes to get the most from the sudden wind shift no matter how exhausted he may be. For example, my competitive effort was heightened during the 1978 Route du Rhum by going to the pulpit each morning and shouting towards the west, where I fancied Malinovsky in his beautiful keelboat might lie, 'One of us multihullers will get you yet', thereby injecting a doctrinaire note into the struggle when I couldn't feel anything but goodwill towards the amiable Michel.

Self-steering – Permission to use electric-powered autopilots, provided their current supply derives from 'wind, waterflow or the sun's rays', was first granted in the 1976 race. A well-engineered device, properly fitted to wheel or tiller, can make or break. Boats slow enough to be controlled by wind vanes will not be in the money in 1980 so they need not be considered here.

Thanks to OSTAR, the design of these battery-powered devices over the past three years has received much attention. The improvements have benefited all yachtsmen, just as the founders of the race had hoped when they originally defined OSTAR's object.

Before the low-demand self-steerer came into being no soloist would have dared to fly a spinnaker of 2,000 square feet from a 60ft hull in 20 knots of wind. Now it's commonplace.

The mention of spinnakers brings to mind a new aid, the Spinnaker Squeezer, a mast-length sock of spinnaker cloth attached to a fibreglass circlet that looks like a top-hat without a crown. Hoisted on the normal spinnaker halyard, its own continuous halyard permits raising and lowering the top-hat so that it frees or furls the spinnaker. It's one more OSTAR spin-off for the good of everyone. Coupled with a good self-steerer, a good squeezer allows the soloist to fly a spinnaker with equanimity.

Weather sense – Understanding the fluctuations of the prevailing westerlies will do much to help a skipper get to Newport first. Eric Tabarly had following air in 1964 when he won his first of two victories. But the other four races have pretty much been sailed on the nose into breezes oscillating from south-west to north-west. Force 1 to Force 5. Now and then the wind drops to nothing or rises to a heavy gale, making the course that much more demanding and taking away any advantage in either a particularly light or especially heavy boat.

The competitors can count on at least one low-pressure system moving from Canada across to Britain at 10-day intervals in June. Its forecasted track and speed will, in the first part of the race, be picked up on British radio, then as the boats cross longitude 40 West from US and Canadian forecasts. With a weather map facsimile receiver, barred in 1976 and again in 1980 but permitted in the 1981 Two-Handed, a skipper might have an advantage in being better able to visualize an approaching storm centre.

The US Navy forecast from Norfolk gives the Gulf Stream co-ordinates daily. Sorting out the most efficient way to cross the Stream in the wind conditions of the moment will give skippers a stimulating intellectual challenge.

The June pilot chart offers little help since its wind roses show only the norms. As Tom Follet, skipper of *Cheers* (third in 1968) and *Three Cheers* (fifth in 1972), will tell you: 'The wind is never normal where you are.'

I've now sailed through the approach area to Nantucket 16 times between May and November. Each time conditions differed. As I gain understanding of how the east-flowing weather from the continent affects the surface winds, the surprises become fewer. But choosing the quickest route will always be a gamble. My recurring nightmare: flat-ass becalmed in thick fog, 50 miles from Brenton Reef, while a pack of front-runners, just to the north, scud before an easterly to erase my lead.

The rules permit communicating with aircraft and ships. Whenever he can, a skipper should ask for the latest forecast on the VHF. There's also the eight-minutes-after-the-hour forecast from WWV, Fort Collins, Colorado, but the guy talks so fast he's hard to transcribe.

Navigation – You'd better be so familiar with sextant and tables you can lay down a sun line-of-position in three minutes, like a robot, no matter how tired or how rough the sea. A pocket calculator will help to give changing Great Circle positions as the race progresses. Are star sights worth the energy expense? Stars would help when closing the coast if the sun has been hidden all day long.

The pilot chart shows the shipping lanes. Expect heavy traffic at their intersections. A radar-warning device can usefully supplement eyesight. It translates the emissions from an approaching ship's radar into a warning signal. Most units of this sort also indicate the direction from which the signal is coming.

The race organizers have supplied each entry with a satellite transmitter. The French pioneered satellite use in an ocean race in the two-handed contest from L'Orient around Bermuda and return, last June. Each time Tyros passes overhead, a signal to a ground-based computer will result in the precise latitude and longitude of each competitor. Double joy. Skippers need no longer worry that their families are worried about their whereabouts; the race sponsors will have a much better chance of engaging media attention for the event.

Costly air/sea searches for the 'overdue' should be a thing of the past. No doubt transmitters will become standard for all ocean-going yachts within a few years.

Conclusion – On Wednesday, 25 June 1980, a trimaran whose skipper managed to achieve all that has been suggested in the foregoing will win OSTAR. This man will have set a new record. But he'd best not get a swollen head because he'll be followed within 24 hours by six other boats, any one of whom might have won had they had his luck.

Singlehanded ocean racing, the most exciting and demanding of all the events on the yacht-racing calendar, will have come of age. Blondie Hasler's visionary concept will have still further advanced the cause of safe, comfortable sailing for everyone.

Relatively few women have entered the Observer Singlehanded Transatlantic Race. Judy Lawson, a well-known American dinghy racer, wrote this piece about arriving at Plymouth to take part in the 1980 OSTAR. Sadly, she was dismasted and had to retire.

ON YOUR MARKS...

Judy Lawson

It is Easter Sunday, 1980, two months and one day before the start of the OSTAR. It is gorgeous, 70-ish and breezy. Everyone in Annapolis is out sailing, except me, a being verging on catalepsy after two days of stocktaking, reorganizing and anguishing over blivets of underwater epoxy (in case the *boat* is holed by a narwhal), circlets of shackles, and baggies of bandages (in case *I* am holed by a narwhal).

Five hundred miles to the north, in another of the East Coast's choice hailing ports, Tom Grossman scrambles for a jangling phone buried beneath a blizzard of paper. 'Who? Whadja say? Call back! – it's a rotten connection. Oh, you. Hey, we're gonna be on television together Tuesday!'

Galvanized with horror (have I lost a day?), I pounce on my calendars. There are three – one for the boat, one for myself, and one for this tiger-by-the-tail of a race. I have been leading three lives. Excuse, please. Sometimes there's a little slippage.

Blessedly, Grossman is wrong. At least my calendar(s) is totally innocent of any Tuesday interview. Though faster than an ICBM, the OSTAR grapevine is as wildly non-accurate and entertaining as Art Buchwald's accounts of the presidential campaigns.

On Tuesday, while Tom is knocking 'em over with unminced ripostes ('Which route am I taking? I didn't know there *were* any routes on the Atlantic. Got a route map I can borrow?') on *Good Morning,*

Left: Denis Gliksman reached Newport in 17th place aboard French entry 'France Loisirs'

America, I will be serenely guiding the president of Serta, Inc., my OSTAR sponsor, on his first visit to the boat.

She has just been launched in her new incarnation as *Serta PerfectSleeper* by the wizard yard, Todd Boat Works in Oxford, Maryland, that has laboured three months to bring forth an OSTAR boat from a Danish day racer. And by the time they trot me out on the tube, Tom will be tearing across the Atlantic towards England.

For an old OSTAR hand like Grossman (fifth overall, second in class in 1976 sailing *Cap 33*), the logistics and organization must be pretty easy. Well, comparatively less frenzied. 'My only problem is money', he says. 'I had to sell the boat yesterday if I'm gonna survive.' *Kriter VII*, Grossman's space-age maxi-tri of the Newick/Bergstrom/Kiwi Boats genre will 'probably be for sale at the finish'.

What's unnerving even the top pros this time is bucks. The way OSTAR works, you got in, committed, and costed it out a long time in advance. Like two to three years ago. (Back in the Golden Age of eight per cent inflation and bearable interest.) Now we are helpless flotsam in the teeth of a hyperinflationary gale. Even the lucky few Americans – by April only Grossman, Rory Nugent, Walter Greene and I – who have attracted commercial sponsors are beggaring ourselves, coldly and deliberately, for the 'privilege' of bashing across the North Atlantic for neither gold nor fame. As Sir Richard Burton wrote when preparing to adventure up the Lower Congo in 1863, 'I ask myself, Why? And the only echo is "damned fool – the devil drives."'

The telephone company's profits rise prodigiously in the final months as the net of long-distance commiseration expands geometrically. We save nickels (phoning during discount times) while swathing our boats in hundreds of thousands of dollars' worth of equipment.

Bear in mind that most of us have never met most of the others, yet we discuss details of our innermost, most private lives (jib hanks, solar cells, fear, food, rage, the state of one's intestines, carbon fibre, dreams, sex, binoculars, bottom paint) for months on end via long-distance phone. We have become members of a family – a family of desperadoes and fugitives from normality. Tough hombres – and terrified ones.

Subtly, we influence each other. For instance, Phil Weld. I had never met the esteemed senior American in the race and godfather of the multihull mafiosi. Somehow, Weld heard that I was planning to ship my boat to England. Weld put out the word that *Lawson was to sail over*. It was only a rumour, a snippet of gossip. A gentle shove

off a cliff. 'Sailing over greatly enhances your pleasure in the race,' he intoned in that wonderful dry, donnish Gloucester voice. 'One becomes practised, you know.'

I sailed.

A stiff south-wester scuds us past storied Eddystone Light. Luminous light on the green hills of Devon limns the boldness of the coast. Inland lies Dartmoor, rugged and brooding, hauntingly beautiful. Midway across the moor, between Newton Abbot and Tavistock, is a dusky pub of memory. Ten years ago . . . Does its ancient clock still tick the seconds Greenwich Mean Time to infinity? Time is a construct for shopkeepers and navigators. The sea and the moor are timeless, but Plymouth is precise. We are required to be logged in at Millbay Dock not later than 1900 hours on 30 May 1980, the rules state, so the OSTAR committees can scrutinize and measure all boats, and, incidentally, fit the Argos satellite transmitters that will leapfrog this race into a televisionary dimension.

Impatiently, we wait for the Millbay lock to open on high water for admittance to the inner sanctum.

Millbay Dock is safe, secure and all but tideless (range less than two feet). It is also inexpensive compared to the stiff marina fees charged elsewhere at Plymouth. It is shunned by the British and the French until the last possible moment before deadline for inspection, I was told by Rory Nugent. We are about to learn why.

'Millbay is one of the few places in the world where you don't have to worry about growth on the bottom,' Nugent said. 'Because there's no oxygen to support life.' The water is an ineffable shade of brown. Dankly drip the stone walls.

At the beginning of the third week in May, all the US boats in Millbay are monohulls. 'Mōnos', as Phil Weld has dubbed us, drawing out the first vowel to a long mournful 'ō'. Or 'one-hullers.'

Why are the multihullers so aggressively defensive? Scratch just a little bit beneath their high-technology surfaces and you learn their risks are shatteringly high. They are the aerialists, the high-wire artists, the early mail pilots of the sea.

As a mōno, I feel a little like a patient who has just been diagnosed as having spring fever, when in the next room they've got plague.

I have a sneaking suspicion that the ballyhooed national rivalries in this OSTAR (Americans form the largest contingent, Britons and French next) are not quite fashionable, hard-nosed nationalism.

Of course, the French may prove me wrong. Nugent has warned that the Tricolor bloc endanger sleep and sanity as the countdown to D-Day grows short. Weld says the French–British rivalry is 'great fun to watch – they're right back in 1066'. Francis Stokes is glad there won't be any force-fed French

Florence Arthaud at the wheel of the unfortunate 'Miss Dubonnet'

monster boats, like *Vendredi 13* or *Club Méd* in this race. No particular reason, 'just glad'.

I am very eager to meet Florence Arthaud, the French 'little mermaid' of La Route du Rhum. At St Georges, Bermuda, last June I watched her sail her big, almost 50ft IOR-style sloop (now renamed *Miss Dubonnet*) into that 'pit stop' for La Transat en Double.

She handled her boat flawlessly, turned around and raced back to France after a couple of hours for repairs and reprovisioning. Having just logged my first solo race (Newport–Bermuda) and feeling fine about the accomplishment, I was bemused with awe. The 635-mile Newport–Bermuda hop seemed suddenly very small spuds.

If bristly rivalries exist – national or other – I am as yet innocent of them, ready to be shocked – or delighted – as Phil Weld has prophesied, by the odd Pole who won't speak to the other odd Pole; by the chest-thumping antics of certain US promoters in cowboy boots; or by Italians covered with cameras taking pictures of other Italians covered with cameras. 'It is', says Weld, 'the most cosmopolitan athletic event of the season.'

Yet the macho-macho bully boy stuff seems insignificant beside the extraordinary (quiet unheralded) help given and received among the OSTAR competitors. No right-minded 'normal' blue-water-racing type would believe it. Perhaps this kind of race brings out the finer qualities in the men who take part in it.

And in the women, one trusts. We are a quartet, the women in the 1980 Race, paired by boat sizes in Pen Duick (James and Arthaud) and Jester (Conners and Lawson) classes. I am sure we will become friends. I am equally sure the press will play upon imaginary distaff rivalries.

Perhaps you have caught a glim of how the whole of a fleet of singlehanders becomes very much more than the sum of its parts. The bonds simply defy discursive descriptions. Having said that, I shall try to describe them – and having failed to describe them, I will confess to a sense of a mystic element ... that solo ocean walloping *feels* like a conspiracy. There is a quantum leap of some kind, and one is never again quite the same. The singlehanded ocean racer is transformed.

Many modern ocean-racing sailors signal each other by their gear: the St David's Light cravats, their discreetly-lettered shirts, a certain pattern of lines around the eyes. Always by vocabulary, a kind of sea-going 'U' and 'non-U' idiom that reeks of Newport, of Antigua, of San Diego or Sausalito or Sydney.

Their common bond is exclusivity. They are a kind of freemasonry, altar boys in the same social church, members of a distinguished club.

Not so the solos. In contrast, what catches the attention is an inability to be 'exclusive' – to see the old distinctions of culture, politics, sex, country, language and physique that separate us in ordinary life. The light is different – or perhaps the view is skewed. Barriers are not dismantled, they are transcended.

There is an account of modern whaling (*Of Whales and Men*) written with great understanding for those who live outside the common herd. In it, a Norwegian whaleman says:

'The motives of some of them are only too painfully obvious – personal glory, kudos, or even material gain. But ... there's always a handful who keep coming down here as it were for the fun of it ... they find something down here which is an absolute necessity if men are to survive, but is rarely met with in other places and conditions – namely, real comradeship. That's a human relationship second only to sexual love, and a thousand times rarer.'

That is also the paradox of the solo sailor.

Phil Weld had told it like it would be – and that was how it was. The only point he had omitted to mention in his prescient article for *Sail* had been the identity of the record-breaking victor: a 65-year-old journalist turned newspaper owner turned passionate multihull advocate called Phil Weld. He had also failed to predict that he would be the first American ever to win. Frank Page, then *The Observer* yachting correspondent, was in Newport to greet *Moxie* and to hear her skipper's own account of the voyage.

THE OLD MAN AND THE SEA

Frank Page

Phil Weld never sets sail to cross an ocean without his trusty Penguin Classic edition of *The Odyssey*. When he sailed majestically into the harbour at Newport, Rhode Island to score his famous victory in the Observer/Europe 1 Single-handed Transatlantic Race, the travel-stained book was lying handily above his chart table.

'I read the chapter on Aeolus like the Gospels', said Weld. 'I have this funny feeling that because I have made such a life-long commitment to the wind, Aeolus is taking heed. It was in his interest that I should be favoured in this race. That's because the causes which I serve are the causes which make him – the Wind King – such an important figure in the Greek pantheon.

'In the Fitzgerald translation of the book he is called the Wind King, not the Wind God. I think that's probably a nice distinction. Like all kings he likes to be flattered.'

As a matter of fact, he gets more than flattery from this old salt. As he skimmed across the Atlantic in his sparkling white trimaran, *Moxie*, the 65-year-old American claims that he was constantly making invocations to Aeolus. 'I am in touch with him all the time, and I'm always thanking him – pulling the forelock and saying, "Anything you choose to give me is far too good for me."'

Weld's not altogether frivolous obeisance clearly gets results. His 51ft yacht sped away from the start of the race in Plymouth three weeks ago and was already well ahead of the fleet by the time it passed the Eddystone Light. He was never headed again

Victorious Phil Weld meets the press at Goat Island

until he creamed across the finish line just outside Newport at breakfast time on Wednesday, slicing an incredible two days and 14 hours off the record which had stood for eight years.

It was a remarkable feat, even discounting the fact that the lean and grizzled Weld was the most venerable competitor in the race. Whatever the benefits of divine intervention, the self-proclaimed acolyte of Aeolus had not merely demonstrated his vast canniness and dedication as a seaman; he had also hustled his vessel across the North Atlantic at more than 200 miles a day to come within an ace of fulfilling his own predictions.

His trimaran crossed the line on the day he had prophesied, after less than 18 days' sailing and only six hours slower than the 425-hour time target he set almost a year in advance. Had he thought then that he might be the skipper of the winning trimaran? 'I thought that *Moxie* was capable of it, but I thought the weak link was me.'

This is not false modesty: Weld's effusive generosity makes him prize others' achievements and abilities much above his own. After his triumph last week he said that if either Alain Colas or Mike

McMullen had survived to enter this year's race with boats as modern and powerful as *Moxie*, they would have been in Newport in time to give me a finish story for *last* week's issue of *The Observer*.

In the same way, when one of the welcoming crowd at Newport referred to his 'great seamanship', Weld insisted on deflecting the compliment. 'I'm an assiduous student', he said. 'For ten years I've been learning from other people: this fleet is filled with my tutors.'

But the irrefutable fact is that it was Weld who beat them all home. It was he who commissioned Dick Newick to design him a light, stiff and fast trimaran. He ordered Hood's, the sailmakers, to rig it with furling headsails and a mainsail which rolls away into the mast. He supervised the building of the boat to include all the latest thinking in sail handling and self-steering gear so that he should be able to sail her to her full potential without exhausting himself.

And it was he who sailed her hard and swiftly along a course perfectly navigated to cover 3,000 miles to Newport as quickly as possible with the least adverse weather.

It was a triumph of intelligent application – the reward for years of planning and pragmatism rather than an explosion of brilliant but risky race techniques.

Weld is the first to admit that he sails his boats conservatively, shortening sail early rather than late when the wind is getting up.

'For the first five and three-quarter days we were going fantastically – close reaching with northerly winds, and I couldn't do anything wrong except go too fast and break the boat up. After that I did wonder why some of my French friends went so far north. I had worked hard on preparing my weather plan and I knew it was imprudent to go above the latitude of 45 North past the longitude of 35 West. So I headed for that corner and stayed on the sunny side of some nasty lows that hit the French right in the teeth.'

'Imprudent' is the sort of unemphatic word which crops up often in Weld's conversation. He used it again when talking about the most dangerous moment of the crossing.

'I was worried about Eric Loizeau and Eugene Riguidel until they had to drop out of the running. Then Jaworski, the Pole, came stealing up on me in his *Spaniel II*, as I was about to head across the Grand Banks south of Newfoundland in fog.

'I thought to myself, "Oh brother, those pros are after me." The visibility was down to about 200 yards and it wasn't blowing more than about 14 knots, but it was at exactly the right angle for me and soon we were going at 20 knots across the Banks, lickety, lickety, lickety, split.

'I was able to take the tension of it for about four hours and then I couldn't stand any more – I reduced sail and slowed down. But I think that I got my lead restored in the time, though it was really the only imprudent thing I did the whole trip.'

So it was a voyage without disasters? 'No disasters at all. The most nearly disastrous thing I could have done would have been to make the wrong guess on the winds and get caught in calms. But the early success put me on my mettle. I kept thinking "You're going to fail your friends if you don't get on with it." And I think I can look Tommy in the eye and say I did not shirk my duty once.'

'Tommy' is Tommy Perkins, a young friend and sailing companion less than half Weld's age, but a tough and aggressive crewman in competitions. 'The best thing I did on the way over for this race was to go to La Trinité in France for the multihull races there. I learned such a lot from watching Tommy, who showed me how easy it was to change up the light Genoa headsail and take it off again. I had always regarded this as a terrifying exercise when sailing alone, just as I did changing the spinnaker. But watching Tommy, I learned a hell of a lot. It made me feel very "up".'

And he was very 'up' when he finished the course on Wednesday, exchanging the solitude of the sea for the welcoming crowd on the quayside. Though the most gregarious of men in port – there were dozens of friends and relations to celebrate his triumph at Newport last week – Weld clearly has a developed appetite for sailing alone. 'Call it the Lindbergh Syndrome,' he says. 'It's all to do with the joy of singularity – when you do something completely on your own abilities and decisions. I enjoy that.'

But was there ever a moment when he had been really frightened? 'No, I promise you that. Not a dry mouth in the whole 17 days – and I've had dry mouths often enough when sailing. My heart just grieved for poor Florence Arthaud when I saw her mast buckle at the start. I was thinking to myself: "What could be more awful than to have your mast break just before the start?" and I decided the only thing worse would be to fall overboard just as you were approaching the finish – to have your boat finish but you not on it.

'That would set a problem for the committee.'

Somebody spoke of the 'boredom' he must have experienced and the answer was a high-pitched but good-natured wail of complaint about just how busy he had been. 'Boredom was never a problem. I've been working a 20-hour day and I had to prepare a schedule of things to do each morning. There were three reports on the race to listen to each day, the BBC weather forecast at a set time, the ham radio network to call – and that's just to begin with.

'Call it the Lindbergh Syndrome. It's all to do with the joy of singularity – when you do something completely on your own abilities and decisions.'

Phil Weld

'Then I had to keep all the movie cameras fed – I've got a sackful of film ready for my producer. And then you've got to worry about working the boat and navigating the course. Some time in all that you have to eat and clean yourself as well. Boredom? Boy!'

Watching him at his press conference drawing disparaging distinctions between the radical racing machines in *The Observer* race and the stately but stultified 12m yachts now tuning up at Newport for the America's Cup in September, it is hard to imagine that boredom has ever been much of an affliction for Phil Weld.

A journalist all his life, his background is New England aristocracy and Harvard. His journalistic career included a period as head of the *Herald Tribune* European bureau in Paris, and many years as a director of the *Boston Globe*. Before he sold it a couple of years ago, he had built up his own thriving chain of newspapers on the north shore of Massachusetts with the same energy and enthusiasm as he now diverts to sailing.

With the same readiness to explore new technology, too. His group was one of the first in the US to use computer typesetting and modern methods of offset printing, and it was always what he calls, appropriately, 'a tight ship' – run with a minimum of staff and maximum of financial benefit.

It is his passion for efficiency that also makes him a committed believer in wind power, who has invested considerable amounts of money in companies dedicated to developing commercial shipping under sail and windmills to generate electricity.

'I believe that we are going to see a breakthrough in the consciousness of shipping people about how well we can employ the wind,' Weld says, 'making use of science to improve the performance of sailing vessels.

'It all came home to me much more forcefully as I was crossing this time, seeing all those oil guzzlers going past, running ever slower and slower because they have to throttle down to save juice. I even overtook a couple of them.'

The sale of the newspaper business meant that he could afford to build his new 51-footer without the need for commercial sponsors and still keep the 60ft *Rogue Wave* in which he finished third in both The Observer Round Britain Race and the French-organized Route du Rhum in 1978.

The very name *Rogue Wave* says a lot about Weld's wry sense of humour. After finishing 27th in the 1972 Observer Singlehanded at the helm of a fast but fragile trimaran called *Trumpeter*, he asked Dick Newick to design a 60ft triple-huller.

She was called *Gulf Streamer* and after finishing third in the 1974 Round Britain Race, Weld took her back to the US by way of the Caribbean. But recrossing the Atlantic before the 1976 Single-handed, she was flipped over by the phenomenon all seamen dread – the monster wave which builds up in a heavy but otherwise benign sea. Weld and his crewman lived for four and half days in the upturned main hull of *Gulf Streamer*, until they were rescued by a freighter.

Totally undeterred by the experience, he first wrote an authoritative article for other multihullers who might have the same experience, full of practical survival advice, then set about building a near replica of *Gulf Streamer* to be called *Rogue Wave*. She was to have been Weld's yacht for this year's race, but the new size limit ruled her out. So *Moxie* was designed by Newick, of course, and built specially.

The name *Moxie* has its story, too. It is taken from a sugar-based tonic drink, originally made in Maine, which Weld remembers from his childhood. The Moxie company still exists, but it does not foot Weld's sailing bills.

The confident claims of the original Moxie label, written in the effusive days of 1876, appeal to Weld's sense of humour. So he distributes specially printed leaflets which remind us that Moxie 'contains not a drop of medicine, poison, stimulant or alcohol. It can recover brain and nervous exhaustion; loss of manhood, imbecility and help-lessness. It gives a durable solid strength, makes you eat voraciously and takes away the tired sleepy lifeless feeling like magic.'

It is very clear that victory in this race, so long one of the skipper's most intense ambitions, did all of that for him.

Aeolus the Wind King has done Phil Weld and
'Moxie' proud. They reached the Brenton
Tower in record time in 1980 and the launches
were waiting to hoot them home

Dick Newick is doyen of the OSTAR designers. A rangy, quiet-spoken New Englander, other multihull designers speak of him as the man who first contrived to make a trimaran look beautiful and all-of-a-piece. His inspiration has produced a whole flotilla of famous OSTAR names. Besides Phil Weld's *Moxie*, victor of 1980, there was *Cheers* (below), *Three Cheers* and Mike Birch's little giant-killer *The Third Turtle*, which came in third behind *Pen Duick VI* and *Club Méditerranée* in the stormy race of 1976. Jim Brown talked to him for *Sail* magazine before the 1980 OSTAR. In 1984, another trimaran man came to the fore, South African-born John Shuttleworth. Trevor Grove met him in Newport as he waited to see how his creations performed – and prospected for future commissions.

DESIGN FOR WINNING

Dick Newick's design philosophy is straightforward but unyielding. 'There are', he says, 'three major requirements that most people want in their boats: large accommodations, low cost, and high performance. I tell my clients that they can choose any two, from a good designer, and be reasonably assured of getting them – but *only* two. In my designs I offer the latter two in combination; *really* high performance at reasonable cost.'

The reasonable cost part was not immediately evident. Most of Newick's better known boats have been custom one-off creations like *Cheers*, *Three Cheers*, and *Gulf Streamer*. Their economy shows only when you compare their cost with that of other vessels on the ocean-racing course. Or when you figure a number that somehow expresses dollars-per-knot.

The Third Turtle for instance showed herself capable of sailing at about the same speed as the competition for about one to two per cent of the cost. 'I like to say', Newick told me, 'that very few of my boats have ever been beaten by anything smaller or cheaper. But just think of what we might accomplish with the budgets of those *big* ones.'

Newick does a fair bit of agonizing over the subjective nature of the word 'performance'. He is turned off by the four-colour advertisements for production rule-boats. These ads rave in print about unspecified speeds which Newick regards as '... painfully limited and sluggish at best. Those guys don't know what the word "performance" means.' I've seen him read these ads, and react with his favourite expletive, a gruffly mumbled 'Oh, *ballast!*'

Even among today's multihulls, Newick is angered by claims of speed and handling which he knows to be deceptive. 'There's just no way to have a high-performance multihull and a roomy, cruising-type accommodation at the same time ... not without the boat becoming very large and costly. All the "room" in a roomy boat just naturally becomes filled up in time with what I like to call *modern inconveniences*, and that means weight. If the boat is heavy, it has to have wide, deep hulls to carry that weight. Wide, deep, heavy hulls just don't go fast – not fast enough to be deserving of the term "high performance" in today's language.'

To this I remarked that some contemporary multihulls (I was thinking of the ones I design myself) must look to him as if their hulls are pumped up like a football.

'Yes, a football,' he grinned, 'a football on the bottom and a football *field* on top.'

Dick Newick, multihull designer:
'There is only one thing we don't have room for
and that is compromise'

By contrast, Newick's designs look like creatures. One night we went through a huge roll of boatplans. The roll of his drawings led me through a detailed examination of just about everything he had ever drawn. At the core of these was his old catamaran, the *Aye-Aye*, which had been the nucleus of his busy charter business in the Virgin Islands for so many years.

There was *Trice* and *Trine* and *Tricia*, all trimarans which logged thousands of safe, profitable and happy miles hauling sun seekers.

Next we thumbed through a grand scrapbook, photos of his early boating involvement. There were kayaks in California, a little Danish double-ender in which he cruised all through Scandinavia, and a dutiful dinghy which he used for transportation in the Sea of Cortez while living with the Seri Indians there.

Referring to his kayaks he said, 'I first learned about boat design from boats that I had to *push* through the water.' Then he returned to the drawings and unrolled an incredible array of catamarans, trimarans and proas.

Ah! The proa, that most mysterious of multihulls – it sails with either end forward. Dick has created several specimens of this unilateral sidecar special, and at his shop (a plastic-covered Quonset in the woods below the house) there is a warning sign over the entrance which reads *Beware! Proa Constructor*.

I was surprised by Newick's willingness to share design information, and amazed by the sheer anatomical inventiveness of his boats. They seem to be the product of eons. Like throw-backs which ran the gamut of natural selection long ago, they have emerged now from Dick Newick's mind absolutely immutable. Their appearance is a bit cold, almost reptilian, yet smug. They stare at you and say, 'I am purely operative ... I need no fat ... my defences are built in ... I am *fast.*'

Newick's design work looks starkly uncomplicated. 'I am a great believer', he says, 'in that old design discipline called KISS: Keep It Simple, Stupid.'

'There is only one thing we don't have room for and that is compromise.' A brochure on his Val class trimaran has a brief statement that describes her interiors. It reads in sharp contrast to the usual designer's rantings about accommodation: 'Two cabins with simple essentials for a couple who appreciate the potential of an easy hundred-mile weekend range.'

I once overheard him talking with a client on the phone. The man had apparently called to ask for more room and Newick responded. 'Do you think I'm going to let your wife design my boat for you?'

JIM BROWN

The designer of 'Fleury Michon' and 'Travacrest Seaway' was actually trained as an electrical engineer. As part of the new technology, he designs with the aid of a computer.

John Shuttleworth wears pink jeans, scuffed sneakers and granny glasses. He has a wispy New Testament beard and long bleached hair. He looks like someone who hit the hippy trail back in the early 1970s, and he did. By then he had already graduated from Cape Town University with distinction, an electrical engineering degree and a passion for computers. But there had been nothing in his life save an interest in surfing and dinghy sailing to suggest that he would one day become one of Britain's top designers of multihull yachts.

As the first four boats across the 1984 OSTAR finishing line came into Goat Island Marina, Shuttleworth stood on the quayside smiling broadly. Not only had he designed *Fleury Michon*, the handsome trimaran that had taken line honours and broken Phil Weld's 1980 record; he was also the designer of *Travacrest Seaway*, which had led the fleet for most of the last week of the race and came in fourth, also shattering the record.

Shuttleworth's first encounter with a trimaran had been back in his native South Africa in 1971, when he helped to crew one across the Atlantic to Brazil. It was a fairly primitive craft by present day standards: 'We had to drag car tyres astern of us to slow the boat down and keep her under control.' But he was hooked. He came to Britain, met his wife and they decided to build a trimaran using a £250 set of plans from Derek Kelsall (designer of Phil Weld's *Trumpeter*). He went to work for Kelsall, and it was then that his computer expertise came into its own.

'The state of the art then was really quite basic. There hadn't been much use of computers for design work and I started playing around predicting performance figures for multihulls on a small computer Derek Kelsall had. Applying physics and mathematics to yacht design was simple for me. Take the way the length of a boat affects its speed, for example. It's really all to do with waves, the waves a boat makes going through the water. Having studied something as complicated as plasma physics, which is also to do with waves, this kind of thing held no fears for me.'

Shuttleworth had helped Kelsall design *Great Britain IV* for Chay Blyth in 1978, and eventually designed *Brittany Ferries* for Chay in 1981 on his own. Chay put his name on the map.

Now Shuttleworth's particular talent for feeding design requirements into a computer and getting out of it race-winning thoroughbreds is so well established that he has been asked to attempt drawing up the rating rules for international multihull racing. It is a delicate undertaking. The very reason that Shuttleworth is so enamoured of multihulls is that 'they are the most unrestricted boats around'.

Comparatively speaking, multihull design is still in its prodigious infancy. Most offshore racing is confined to monohulls, though the enthusiasm for unrestricted contests pioneered by races like OSTAR is now gathering momentum worldwide, especially among the French. In these sorts of races it is increasingly clear that monohull boats are falling behind the multihulls, and that the principal design effort is going into the latter.

'The days of the enthusiast with no money — which is how the multihull movement started – are over,' says John Shuttleworth, 'and not only because of sponsorship.' He sees a whole new era coming when the ordinary cruising sailor will opt for the higher performance, greater stability and more generous deck space of trimarans. 'Capsizing is still a problem. But there is a huge amount of work going into self-righting.'

Meantime, however, it is the big racing machines that preoccupy him and rival designers such as Nigel Irens, creator of *Lada Poch*. The overriding need for speed, while offsetting strength against weight and buoyancy against drag, is a constant challenge.

'There is actually more similarity in many ways between a racing mono and a racing multi,' says Irens, 'than there is between a racing boat and a cruising boat with the same number of hulls.'

There is quite a lot of plagiarism at the sharp end of the design duel. 'Fear of making mistakes encourages us to communicate with each other', Irens points out. And in the end they are all tussling with the same problems: not the least of which is money.

'When I have fed everything else into the computer, I then have to put in the economic requirements', says Shuttleworth. 'These are absolutely crucial.' Making catamarans wider, for example, might give one a steadier, faster platform and reduce the risk of a capsize, but one has to consider that the modern materials required to make a big, broad catamaran stiff enough to sustain all that rigging through pounding seas are bound to cost that much more money.

John Shuttleworth saves part of his costs by doing almost all his testing with small radio-controlled models out on the Solent and also on the computer itself.

'Computers are outdating tank and wind-tunnel testing. A big one can simulate every kind of condition far more accurately and cheaply. Southampton University's tank, for example, costs £1,000 a time. On my computer I can actually work out how much stress a trimaran float will have to endure in its whole lifetime. I can calculate how many waves it will bang into.' (The answer is in millions, but he won't say how many.)

Meanwhile, however, as the designers juggle with their parameters and the speed records tumble like masts in a hurricane, the basic problems that confront small boats in big oceans remain stubbornly unimpressed. Halyards part, hulls hit whales, Genoas split, skippers fall down or asleep or overboard.

The real limits on the designer's art are not just the technology but, as always, the man and the weather and the unpredictable sea.

TREVOR GROVE

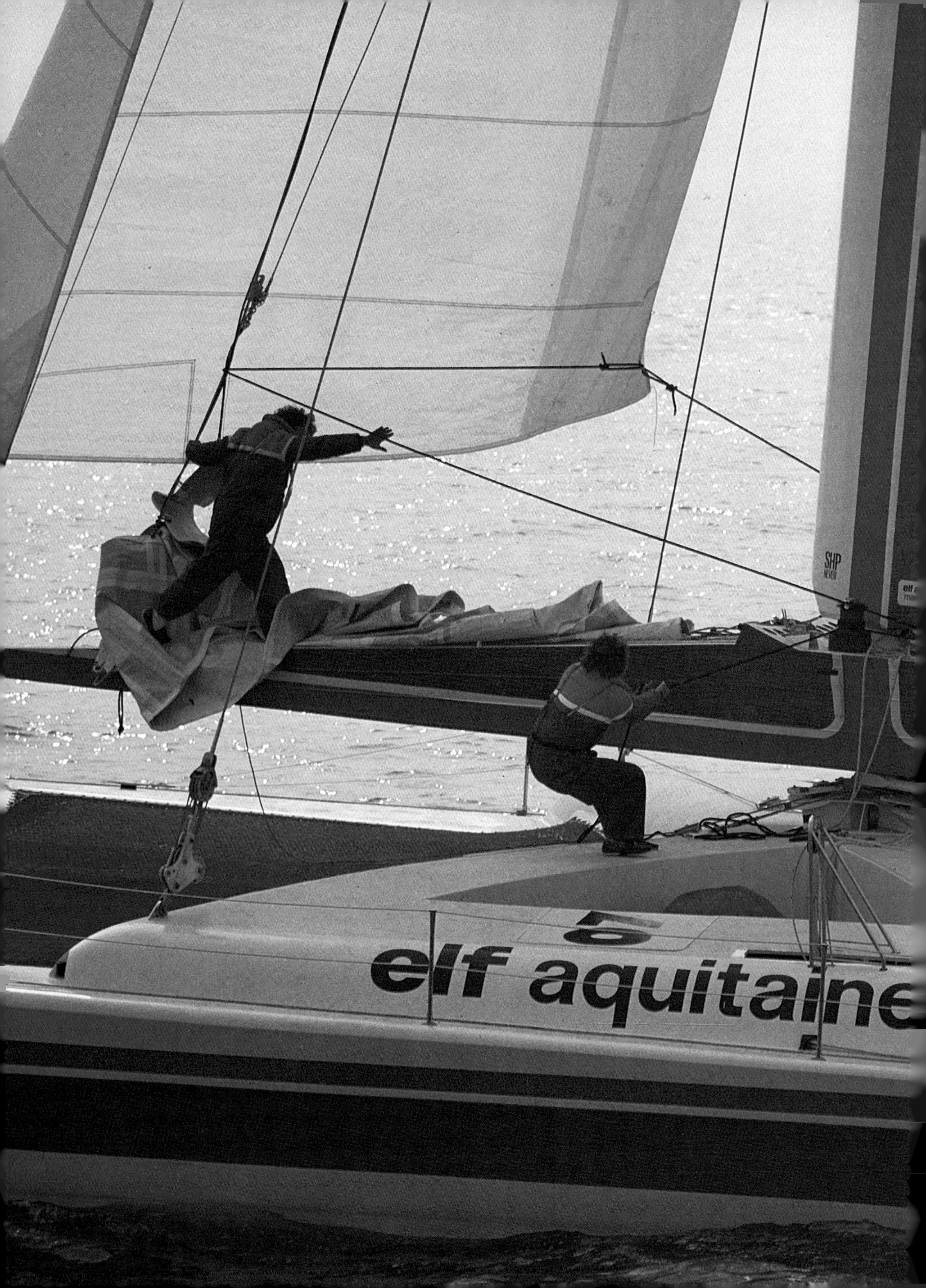
elf aquitaine

When Blondie Hasler conceived the idea of racing across the Atlantic singlehanded one of his motives was to encourage innovation in yacht design. His intention has proved successful. The OSTAR legacy can today be discerned in almost every new yacht that leaves a boatyard. Geoff Hales, a yachting journalist and consultant who specializes in technological matters and is himself an OSTAR veteran, has charted that achievement.

HI TECH ON THE HIGH SEAS

Geoff Hales

There is a view, fortunately not shared too widely, that as the father of single-handed ocean racing OSTAR has been an irresponsible parent. Bigger and bigger boats have been encouraged to go faster and faster, posing a danger not only to their own one-man crews, but, worse, to innocent small craft that might get in their way.

What tends to be ignored by such critics is the enormous contribution the race has made over the years not only to speed and efficiency at sea, but to the ease and safety of yachting in general. Devices pioneered by the Observer sailors are now standard equipment on cruising boats all over the globe. No longer does a skipper have to find a beefy crewman before he sets off for a weekend sail: with the aid of up-to-date steering gear and winches and sail-handling systems his wife or children will be all the crew he needs. Navigation has become more accurate. Yachts are stronger and lighter, thanks to new materials. Multihulls have become less prone to the catastrophe of a capsize. A racing machine like *Elf Aquitaine* or *Paul Ricard* might well look more at home on a rocket launch pad than in a yacht marina, but just as NASA's space programme has had uncounted benefits for the ordinary house-holder, so the OSTAR spin-off is evident wherever small boats are built and sailed.

Back in 1960, when the race began, the funda-mental problem was simply getting the boat to steer itself. Photographs of Francis Chichester's *Gipsy Moth III* always show a big wind vane aft, a bit like a small sail. This was Miranda, and Chichester merely harnessed her up like a weather cock to the steering system, allowing the wind direction to control the rudder. The trouble was he needed a fairly dramatic shift in the wind before Miranda actually pulled the tiller very far. And the pressure on the vane had to be fairly strong, hence the large size of Miranda's wing.

Blondie Hasler realized that there was a better way of doing this, using the power of the water running past the hull to provide assistance. He geared a much smaller wind vane so that it simply altered the angle of a slim servo blade under water. The pressure of the water against the blade was

then used to work the tiller, with considerable force.

It's fair to say that without the impetus of solo racing, the self-steering gears which yachtsmen take for granted today would never have achieved their present level of efficiency and reliability. Paralleling this evolution, however, has been the development of electronic steering systems, designed to follow a set course rather than simply keep the boat at a certain angle to the wind. In any case, wind vane gears were never so effective off the wind and could go positively haywire in the case of the big fast multihulls that were emerging from the OSTAR designers' drawing boards. These vessels could accelerate at such a velocity that they changed the relative angle of the wind very quickly. Vane steering gears simply couldn't cope with this. The faster the boats went, the more urgent the require-ment to be able to set the helm on a compass course and keep it there.

Electric autopilots had been around for years, but they were cumbersome and power-consuming. Thanks to the impetus of singlehanded racing new lightweight versions using minimal power have been developed which can also be used when motoring.

To make these low consumption autopilots suitable for even the fastest multihulls, the power of the water rushing past the hull is harnessed once again. This time the autopilot operates a trim tab on the back of the rudder. The tab's movement forces the main rudder to move and steer the boat.

Best of all are the new generation of self-steering systems, such as Peter Phillips had on *Travacrest* and after which he named his boat. They combine a choice of both wind vane and electronic power, with the aid of a microcomputer. Such a device would have been inconceivable five years ago, never mind in 1960 when it all began.

Just as remarkable have been the navigational innovations. Until 1980, the only aids permitted by the rules were the sextant, radio direction-finding equipment and a depth sounder. This meant that the art of navigation was crucial to success in the

Highest hi tech: previous page, 'Elf Aquitaine' with extra crew; opposite, 'Club Méditerranée'

Old and new: above, 'Paul Ricard's revolutionary foils; below, Chichester hanks on a pre-self-furling foresail

race. But that particular constraint proved harder and harder to police and was eventually lifted. As a result a lot of boats these days not only have visible radar scanners but can, down at the chart table, tune into satellite navigation systems that will provide an accurate fix every 40 minutes or so on average. However, when you really want one, the chances are you will have to wait three hours. This is just one example of 'Sod's Law of Sailing'.

Once upon a time, such exotic equipment was prohibitively expensive. I hired a satnav 10 years ago. The unit was the size of a refrigerator, it produced its answers on pieces of punched paper tape and it made a sound like a cash register. We needed it for a commercial project and it cost us £40,000 for eight months' use. Today a satnav receiver would cost about £1,000 to buy outright.

It was partly the cost that had stopped the Royal Western allowing such equipment in earlier races: cost and bulk, both of which presented insuperable problems for unsponsored skippers at the smaller end of the fleet. Back in 1968 it had been thought unfair that Geoffrey Williams and *Sir Thomas Lipton* had benefited from a shore-based weather computer. In 1976 Alain Colas was prevented from using satnav aboard his colossal 236ft *Club Méditerranée*. Now, however, satnav is only one of the new navigational systems that might fit the average

The Argos System

Singlehanded ocean racing is a dangerous sport. As the pressure to win becomes greater, the sailors push their boats harder and harder. The organizers, the Royal Western Yacht Club, while continuing to encourage the spirit of adventure, feel that closer control is necessary for the safety of competitors, and to this end, in 1980, they began to use the Argos system of satellite plotting of the boats' positions.

Each of the competing yachts is fitted with a balise containing a platform transmitter terminal (PTT). The signal from this is picked up by two American weather satellites, NOAA 7 and NOAA 8, and directed to one of three ground stations – Gilmore Creek in Alaska, Wallops Island in Virginia, or Lannion in France – depending on the path of the satellites and the relative positions of the boats to their trajectory angle. This information is collected at the National Environmental Satellite Service Center at Suitland, Maryland, before being transmitted to the Toulouse Space Centre where the CNES Service Argos Data Processing Centre is located.

From Toulouse the information is sent to Paris where it is picked up by British Telecom's International Packet Switching Service and transmitted to Wang computers at the race centres in Plymouth and Newport. These carry modified software packages that rapidly deliver the position of each boat in the race and put them in order according to their distance from Newport.

Each of the Argos balises has a 'thumbprint' to identify the individual boat and, in addition, a 'panic button'. Should any skipper run into trouble, he may press the button to activate an emergency signal which will show immediately the next satellite pass is processed. Two of the signals from the balise show temperature and pressure, and these go to maximum reading when the panic button is operated. This is immediately obvious from the Wang computer print-out.

The effectiveness of the system has been proved. In early races some PTTs stopped transmitting because their cases were not properly waterproofed, but after this fault was rectified eight men were rescued from four yachts during the Observer/Europe 1 doublehanded race in 1981. When Ian Johnstone's trimaran capsized in the Route du Rhum the following year, it was the Argos plots that helped the organizers in Paris direct Olivier Moussey, a fellow competitor, to the rescue.

Even more dramatic proof of the importance of the device was provided in the BOC singlehanded round-the-world race when Jacques de Roux pushed his panic button 2,000 miles west of Cape Horn. The race headquarters used a ham radio net to send Richard Broadhead nearly 400 miles to the rescue. As Broadhead's satellite navigation system was not working, the race organizers used the positions the Argos system was giving for both boats to direct him to a successful rendezvous. Less than four hours later, the PTT on Roux's boat stopped transmitting, indicating that it had sunk.   BOB FISHER

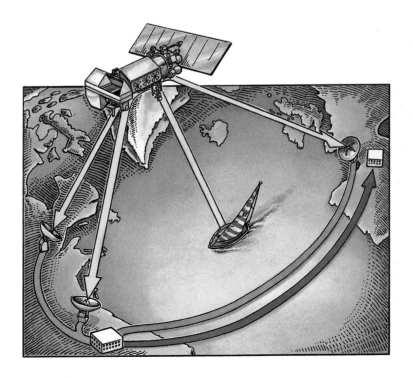

Neco autopilot aboard 'Wild Rocket'

Inside steering station on 'Spaniel'

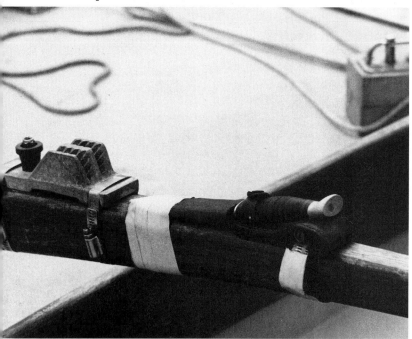

Sheath knife on 'Galloping Gael's tiller

Toe-hold on Mike Kane's 'Spirit of America'

Modern navigation display in 'Patricia of Finland'

TV monitors 'Club Méditerranée's masts

Hasler wind vane steers wheel by means of a pulley

Main outside steering wheel on 'Club Méditerranée'

skipper's yacht as well as his or her pocket.

There are Loran receivers which give continuous fixes within 500 miles or so of the US coast, and Decca receivers which do the same off the UK coast. There is an expensive global system called Omega, and latterly a Racal Decca unit which is capable of monitoring all the other systems at once and outputs a position continuously. It costs £8,000. Incredible, very clever, and, for what it does, inexpensive.

As well as navigating towards a target, there is the more immediate problem of navigating away from intervening obstacles. In the early days, when we did four to six knots if we were lucky, a skipper could afford an hour's sleep fairly confident that he wouldn't be run down before he next looked out of the hatchway. I generally sleep for between half and three-quarters of an hour at a time. I have done the mathematics and calculate that for me to be run down requires a ship to come over the horizon just after my head has hit the pillow, to be travelling in exactly the right direction and at about 16 to 20 knots. With fuel costs as they are, that's slightly less likely than it used to be.

But in the case of a modern racing multihull, capable of sprinting at 25 knots and faster, the dangers are far more acute, even though most singlehanders slow down to sleep. Radar is the

THE CLASSES, 1984

The entrants are divided into five classes (see diagrams, right) and three main types: the familiar, orthodox monohulls; catamarans – twin hulls linked by a bridge deck which carries the mast and sails; and trimarans – triple-hulled craft which sail with the centre hull and one float in the water, the third 'flying' free

Class 1: over 45ft to 60ft

Class 2: over 40ft to 45ft

Class 3: over 35ft to 40ft

Class 4: over 30ft to 35ft

Class 5: over 25ft to 30ft

Above: Warren Luhrs, whose performance in 'Thursday's Child' (1984) brought new hope to monohull supporters, in his gimballed navigating chair. Below: Geoff Hales, singlehander and writer on sailing technology

Above: Peter Phillips had a Travacrest navigational system, complete with microcomputer, aboard his 1984 trimaran. Below: Bill Doelger aboard 'Edith'. Overleaf: Multihull might, the 1980 entry 'Mattia III'

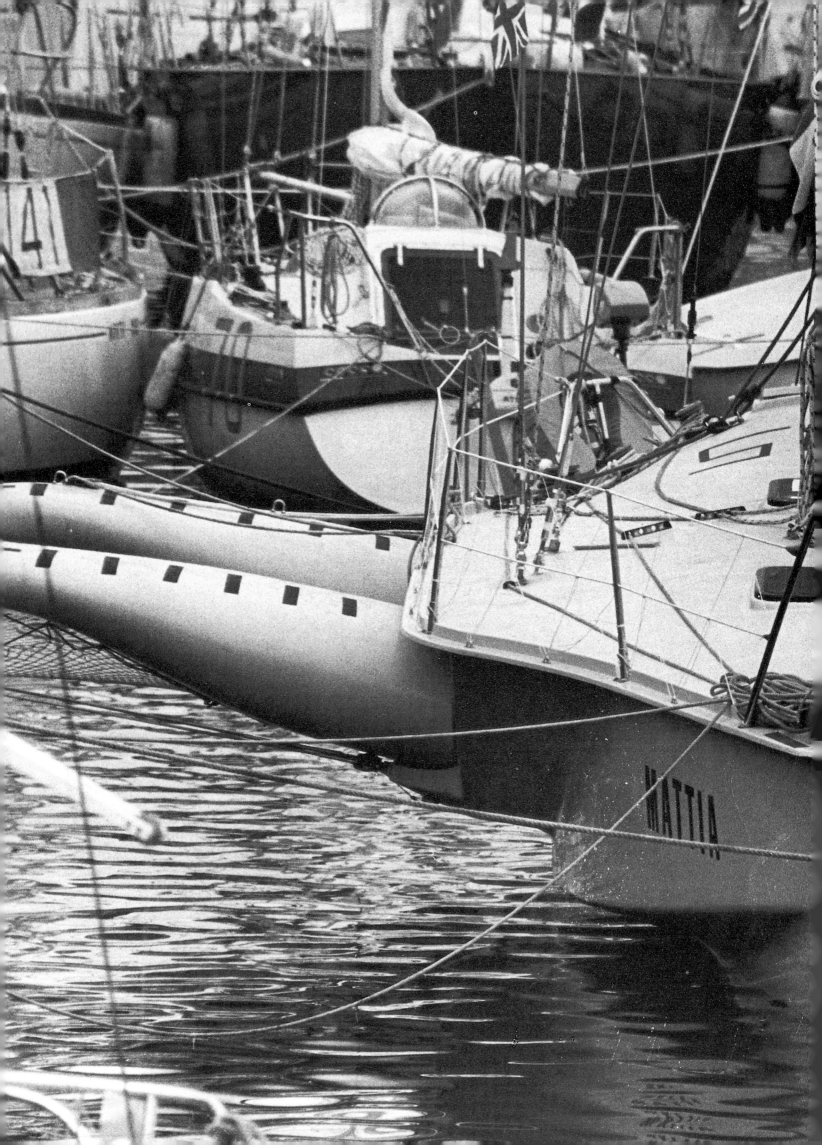

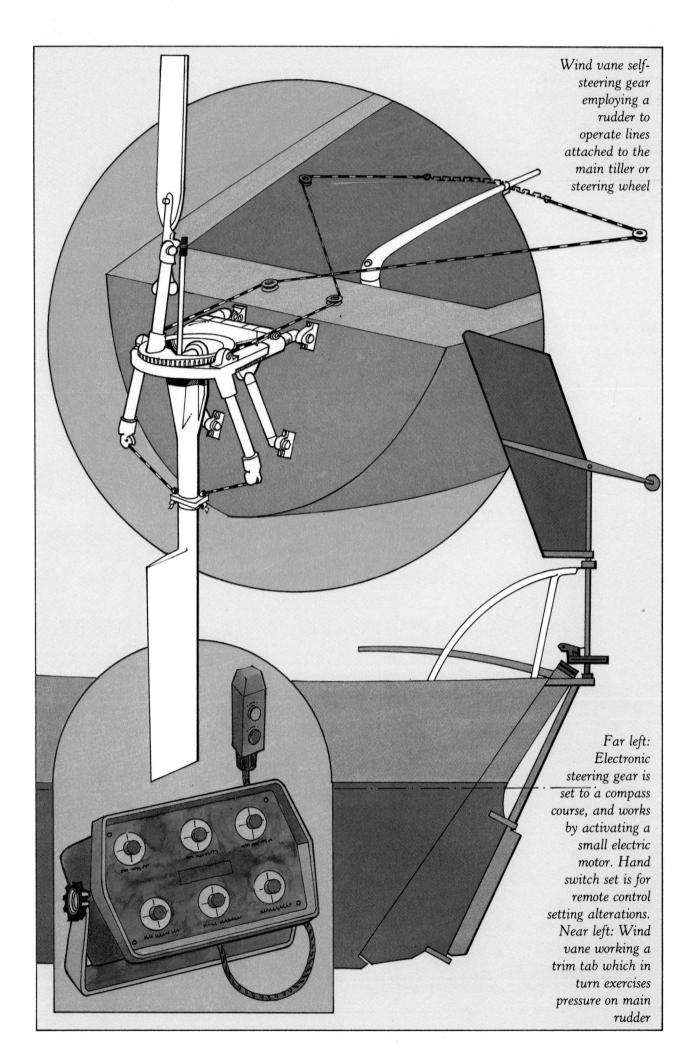

Wind vane self-steering gear employing a rudder to operate lines attached to the main tiller or steering wheel

Far left: Electronic steering gear is set to a compass course, and works by activating a small electric motor. Hand switch set is for remote control setting alterations. Near left: Wind vane working a trim tab which in turn exercises pressure on main rudder

obvious answer. But it needs to have a highly sensitive – and expensive – alarm system. The alternative is a radar detector, which sounds an alarm and provides a bearing when it senses incoming radar signals. That, of course, depends on the approaching vessel having its radar switched on in the first place. But I have used a detector for eight years and wouldn't go to sea without it.

All these electronic aids, needless to say, put considerable strain on the batteries, a problem which the early OSTAR sailors didn't encounter at all. Since the rules of the race used to insist that only the domestic-use batteries might be recharged by means of the engine, great ingenuity has gone into wind and water-powered generators. The latter pose obvious drag problems, the former are prone to damage. The most popular form of energy-gathering in the 1984 OSTAR seemed to be solar panels, their honeycomb patterns appearing on cabin roofs, trimaran outriggers and catamaran bridge-decks even in quite exposed positions: a tribute to the fact that they are far less vulnerable to corrosion or being trod upon than they used to be, though they are slippery underfoot.

So much for steering and navigation, then, areas where OSTAR innovations have plainly been to the advantage of all sailors. More open to debate are the relative merits of the new-fangled boats that the competitors actually sail. Back in 1960 *Gipsy Moth III* was considered too big for a singlehander to manage efficiently. Sails were too large, winches too cumbersome it was said. Such doubts have long since evaporated, partly because of new equipment, partly because the greed for speed has simply forced competitors to work harder than used to be thought possible or prudent.

In point of fact, it has not always been the biggest boat in OSTAR that has won. But since it is broadly true that the potential speed of a yacht is governed by its length, the trade-off between size and manageability has always been a focus for discussion and experimentation. One has to remember that it is easier to sail a 40ft boat at 90 per cent efficiency than it is to sail an 80-footer at perhaps 60 per cent efficiency.

Nevertheless, it is also the case that the bigger the boat is, the less prone it is to be slowed down by the North Atlantic weather, a crucial consideration which is just one of the reasons why OSTAR racers were getting larger and larger until a length limit was imposed in 1980.

Now the goal is to get maximum speed within the maximum length. Monohulls, for example, have come a long way from their traditional cruising image. Their designers have gone for less and less underwater area, in order to reduce drag. Tabarly's *Pen Duick II* back in 1964 was not only the

first boat to be designed specially for this race but also the first to move in the direction of the long-hull, low-drag, small-rig formula. Others have gone for long, thin boats with very tall rigs and very deep keels to balance them, though these have tended to pitch a lot.

Others still have tried to get away from the length/speed deadlock with wider, lighter mono-hulls, theoretically capable of planing, held up against the wind by the use of water ballast. The

Above: First steps in self-steering: Chichester's 'Miranda' gear. Overleaf: Wind vane self-steering in action. OSTAR has enormously influenced the evolution of such gear

width is necessary for leverage to make the water ballast work, and wide boats are not necessarily all that good to windward. Nevertheless, the whole water ballast concept is extremely attractive, because you can put it where you want it, pump in only as much as you need and dump it as soon as you wish. The fact that Warren Luhrs in *Thursday's Child* broke the record (set by Phil Weld's trimaran in 1980) and came in among the multihull leaders in 1984 said everything that needed to be said about

Rory Nugent aboard a proa in Martha's Vineyard. The type was banned in the 1984 race. Below: 'Gautier'

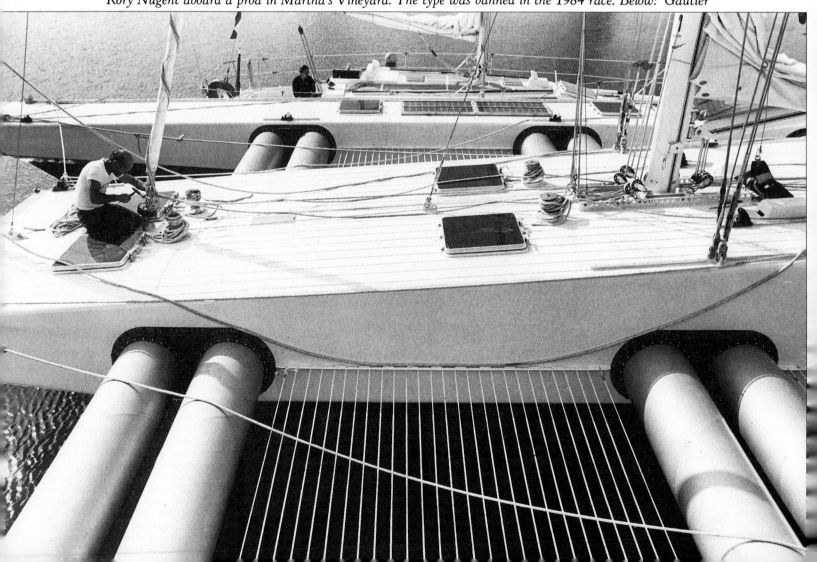

the refinements that are still possible within the traditional single-hulled keel boat concept.

Meanwhile multihullers have also taken to using water ballast to counteract their proneness to get pushed around too much in choppy seas. Even the uncomplicated catamaran I was sailing had a water tank in each hull. I was able to pump water from the lee hull into the windward hull in order to stiffen her and carry more sail.

So here is a fairly typical case of an OSTAR-inspired innovation having an unexpected bonus for others of the sailing fraternity: a technique devised to make monohulls faster being adapted to make multihulls steadier. No doubt such exchanges will continue to occur between designers so long as this race is run and so long as the rivalry between mono-men and multi-men maintains its excitement.

The multihulls, for instance, have also borrowed the long, thin hull idea, multiplying it by three in the case of trimarans. At first the typical tri had rather small, low buoyancy floats and if the wind started to force the leeward float under, you eased up. Now the fashion has moved in favour of more buoyancy in the outriggers, which can make the boat faster and more stable but can also mean that in a strong blow you can lift the whole main hull out of the water, and it all starts to rotate around the buoyant lee hull. There's very little warning of this happening. I have done it in *Travacrest Seaway* with her designer, John Shuttleworth, aboard and he was the only person who had the experience and knowledge of the boat to deal with it. Normally that sort of session ends in a capsize. One of the likely developments of future OSTARs, therefore, could be a design breakthrough that would reduce this danger, just as breakthroughs in new construction materials have led to a revival of the catamaran as a transatlantic racer.

The latest shapes here are very long, very thin hulls that slice through the waves rather than pitch across them, and are smoothed off to reduce the serious problem of wind resistance at speeds of 20 knots-plus. For stability, the hulls are set widely apart. These extraordinary configurations would be impossible but for the strength and lightness of new construction materials such as carbon fibre. To ensure only the required amount of material is used and the maximum strength is obtained from it, now it is even possible to 'tack' the hull fabric together, put the whole structure in a large oven and bake it to produce the finished hull. Previously, it was extremely difficult to mount the mast on a cross-beam and the forestay on another beam and still keep a racing rig taut, because the whole vessel would twist so terribly: it simply couldn't be built stiff enough. Although no cruising catamaranophile would wish to emulate Marc Pajot's tubular living quarters in

the narrow hulls of *Elf Aquitaine*, the success of that extraordinary vessel with her wing mast as wide as a barn door undoubtedly marked the start of a new era for catamaran designers.

One exciting brand of boat that did not put in an appearance in 1984 was the proa. These single-outrigger craft, which reverse their direction rather than tacking (because the float must always be kept to leeward), are tricky to rig and sail, hence the

One way to generate power is to use a windmill ...

... another is to use solar cells, though they are slippery

Royal Western have banned them from single-handed races. But they can be exceptionally fast, as Tom Follett proved in the Dick Newick-designed *Cheers* back in 1968. And they will undoubtedly be back in OSTAR one day.

Another radical direction in which designers have already started to move and are gaining increasing confidence is the use of foils to help provide lift. For the present, these angled blades

Marc Pajot at the helm of 'Paul Ricard' in 1980, sailing as an unofficial entry. The design seems peculiarly ungainly compared with 'Paul Ricard's 1984 successor

Warren Luhrs's monohull 'Thursday's Child' has all the mod cons, including water ballast and cockpit-led lines

tend to be seen on trimaran outriggers such as *Paul Ricard*. There is considerable argument about the amount of drag they cause, but it is clearly a line of experiment that will be pursued in years to come.

There has been only one dead-end from the design point of view in the course of the Observer race, and that was the road towards sheer, overwhelming size. *Vendredi 13* and in the following race *Club Méditerranée* proved pretty conclusively that enormous length and highly sophisticated sail-handling techniques could together make a formidable combination. Who knows where that might have led had the Royal Western not decided that in the interests of sport and safety a length limit

Self-tailing winches, pioneered by solo sailors, are now a boon to all short-handed yachtsmen

should be imposed – 56ft in 1980, 60ft in 1984, though the French have recently been agitating for it to be increased to 85ft.

(The French obviously have a particular passion for monster yachts. In singlehanded races they like to go out to the start with a considerable crew aboard to get the boat started up and pointed in the right direction before leaving her to her skipper at the last possible moment. If the support boat can't keep up the extra crew simply bail out over the side and wait to be picked up.)

Whatever the actual limit of these racing boats, even 56ft, they are still very big vessels and need very big rigs to make them go at racing speeds. And big rigs are tricky to control.

A key development in recent years has been the use of novel sail materials such as Kevlar and Mylar – immensely tough, capable of being rolled round a self-furling forestay and with very smooth surfaces that allow the wind to jet off in the right direction rather than 'stick' to the sail.

Roller furling itself is one of the major benefits to yachting to have emerged from solo racing. No really competitive skipper bothers with hoisting and lowering different sails on the foredeck these days – it can all be done with the aid of a revolving forestay which takes in or pays out the headsail as required and can be controlled entirely by a line leading back to the cockpit. The sail may be a less

Self-furling foresail: cockpit operated line rolls the sail around a rigid steel forestay

Self-furling mainsail: sail is hauled in or out on a roller inside the hollow mast

efficient shape as a result; there may be annoying wrinkles. But the time lost through wrinkled sails is very much less than the time expended through having to change sails completely every time there is a variation in the course or the weather.

Other ingenious techniques for handling sails have been evolved by singlehanders and exploited by quick-thinking commercial manufacturers. There are devices like socks which can be pulled down around a spinnaker to collapse and furl all that billowing gaudiness with the minimum of fuss. There are methods of rolling spare sails onto spare stays, ready for instant rigging. There are special foredeck sail bins into which the forestays descend so that extra sails can be hanked on in advance while keeping the deck uncluttered.

Even the mast can be rotated, as on Phil Weld's *Moxie*, as a means of shortening the mainsail, though this has not proved such a popular invention: the risks of a jam and the difficulty of controlling the sail shape have told against it. In other respects, however, mainsail control has come a long way thanks to carbon fibre battens, slab reefing and laced-up pockets of extra sail area which can be unloosed once the intricate manoeuvrings of the start no longer pose the threat of an ultra-large main fouling the backstay.

In the course of trying to achieve easier sail handling, unconventional rigs have also been given very thorough testings in the Observer race. Blondie Hasler's famous junk rig on *Jester* was still doing good service 20 years after the inaugural OSTAR, with Michael Richey at her helm. Though not very effective in performance terms, it had the singular advantage of being entirely controllable without the necessity of going on deck. New versions of that rig, including a system called a swing wing, are still coming off the drawing-boards.

Surprisingly, the 'freedom' rig has made only one appearance so far. Reminiscent of a wind surfer's set-up, with a wishbone boom, it has proved immensely easy to handle but so far has not shone in light winds. But with the stimulus of OSTAR, we can expect to see improvements in the rig over the next few years.

The same could be said for self-tailing winches and cockpit-led controls – in short, for an enormous and impressive list of ideas that have sprung from the most demanding and unrestricted singlehanded race in the yachting world. OSTAR is a designer's charter. It is not only the ultimate test of speed. It is also a proving ground for reliability, for handling qualities, for efficiency and for safety, a proving ground recognized all over the globe. Not a bad achievement for a race which began with just seven entrants, a half-crown bet and a self-steering gear called Miranda.

Millbay Dock:
a boat show of bizarre variety, with a pleasing
edge of high drama. Here is 'Fleury Michon',
her Argos transponder clearly seen astern of the
cockpit, moored next to 'Roger & Gallet', which
failed to finish the 1984 course

1984

The essence of singlehanded yacht racing, at any rate for the onlooker, is its unpredictability. OSTAR is a bookie's nightmare. Knowing the form of every boat and the track record of every skipper is a help; but few of those who had crowded the Millbay quaysides would hazard a specific forecast. Those who did, confined themselves to saying that the winner would be a multihulled boat, almost certainly skippered by one of France's famous four: Marc Pajot, Patrick Morvan, Eric Tabarly or Philippe Jeantot.

They were right about the nationality, and the first boat across the line was indeed a trimaran. But in every other respect the race turned out to be wonderfully (or in some cases woefully) unexpected. A week from the finish even the near-certainty of a Gallic victory hung in doubt: Jeantot was out of the race, a fault in *Crédit Agricole*'s water-ballast system having caused a capsize; Morvan's *Jet Services*, speeding ahead of the fleet, had rammed a tree trunk; and now Britain's Peter Phillips was actually in the lead ..: That proved to be a false hope when *Fleury Michon* careered over the Brenton Reef to break Phil Weld's 1980 record by 35 hours – and then break her skipper's heart when he learnt, later, that Jeantot's mid-Atlantic rescuer Yvon Fauconnier was the winner on corrected time.

This was by no means the whole of the drama, however. Consider the startling fact that Pajot and his ocean spaceship *Elf Aquitaine* crossed the line just 23 minutes behind Philippe Poupon – the closest finish ever. And Warren Luhrs's astonishing feat in bringing a monohull yacht home within the previous record was a triumph which has put the old mono/multi rivalry back into the centre of the

Left: 'Fleury Michon' 'dead in the water' a day from Newport

ring. More excitements were to follow: Chris Butler's Class V victory for Britain in *Swansea Bay* for example. And Rachael Hayward running aground just six miles from the finish and eliminating the last hope of a woman completing the course: Florence Arthaud had had to scratch *Biotherm II* only halfway across.

Biotherm's upset was not the only case of structural failure. More than a quarter of the fleet failed to finish, a ratio which will have caused some hard thinking by the race committee. This was not a re-run of 1976, after all. The weather was forgiving. Yet even allowing for encounters with logs, straying buoys and playful whales, the toll was still surprisingly high. As Murray Sayle wrote in *The Spectator*, 'rudders failed, hulls cracked and nearly a dozen masts collapsed, despite the claimed use of the most modern materials. On this showing the Spanish Armada would barely have made it out of Cadiz Bay, much less put Plymouth on the international bowling circuit'.

This is all the more puzzling when one considers that all the entrants had done long qualifying journeys aboard their craft, and also submitted themselves to rigorous inspection for seaworthiness. Once again, no doubt, questions will be raised about the wisdom of the OSTAR enterprise. And once again, nonetheless, the spirit of this marvellous, strenuous, occasionally foolhardy, always demanding race will prevail. Wherever small craft try to race so fast and so far, with so few rules to restrict the fearlessness of their skippers and the daring of their designers, accidents will happen, weak links will give. But that is the point of the race, after all: to arrive at the ideal balance between speed and safety, endurance and acceleration, wakefulness and exhaustion. That is precisely the challenge and the allure of the toughest singlehanded sailing race in the world.

Since Tabarly's win in 1964, the Observer Singlehanded Transatlantic Race has attracted a strong French field. Now that their radio station Europe 1 has become co-sponsor, France's solo sailors are even keener to compete. In 1984 *The Observer*'s distinguished sports writer Hugh McIlvanney backed a 32-year-old Breton, Philippe Jeantot. In the event, Jeantot came to grief. But who could have foreseen that outcome a week before the race?

BRETON HOPES

Hugh McIlvanney

There are some among our English-speaking fraternity so unenamoured of being beaten by the French that they like to believe Harold the Saxon lost that fight at Hastings in 1066 on a dubious cut-eye decision. Nonetheless, the French have come to conquer, as single-minded about winning the race as William the Conqueror was about winning a new kingdom.

Some feel that the most famous of their 20-odd contenders, Eric Tabarly, the brilliant, unbreakably determined sailor who won the second Observer transatlantic race from Francis Chichester in 1964 – he did it again in 1976 – and kindled an enthusiasm that has given his country pre-eminence in ocean racing two decades on, will become a largely nostalgic figure. But that is a hazardous assumption to make about a man so conspicuously resistant to the softening effects of middle age. Even Tabarly himself, however, may expect to see a younger Frenchman towing the fleet into Newport one day. It could be Patrick Morvan or Marc Pajot, in big, fast catamarans. But the cat that takes the cream in the end may be *Crédit Agricole*, the 60-footer sailed by Philippe Jeantot, a 32-year-old Breton with fair claims to being the most inspired newcomer this form of competitive yachting has ever known. Jeantot had never competed solo in his life when he entered the round-the-world race sponsored by the BOC Group in the late summer of 1982. Admittedly, 25,000 miles of singlehanded sailing had provided him with decent practice, but nobody was prepared for what he did to his 16 opponents in the BOC Challenge. What he did was slaughter them. By the end of the first leg, from Newport to Cape

Preceding pages: Philippe Jeantot's 'Crédit Agricole' at speed. Stability remains a problem even for this generation of monstrously wide catamarans

Town, he was 1,200 miles ahead of his nearest pursuer and he was fastest over all three subsequent legs of the race. He returned to Newport 11 days and 14 hours before the second man home and most people in the sport accepted that even the excellence of his boat (*Crédit Agricole* was then a powerful 56ft monohull) counted for less than the skill and originality with which he handled her.

Jeantot was by no means the only competitor in the BOC who relied extensively on modern electronic equipment, but he used it far more boldly and to much greater effect than the others. For instance, he carried a radiofacsimile weatherchart printer and had enough faith in what it told him about the whereabouts of winds and storms to ignore the generalized recommendations contained in the standard guide on the best routes, *Ocean Passages for the World*. That huge lead he established between Rhode Island and Cape Town owed much to his decision to sail straight between two hurricanes. 'I had the same books the other navigators had but I would think, "That book was written one century ago when the clippers were sailing." The clippers were very heavy, not good for tacking. Our boats are very different, so the routes should be different. Going between those hurricanes was a risk, but the weather facsimile told me it was not a bad risk. When I sail I calculate the percentages, as I did when I was a diver.'

Philippe Jeantot was indeed a diver, such a remarkable practitioner of that dangerous trade that he was included in the team of six that set a depth record of 1,640ft in 1977 while connecting pipes on the sea-bed off Toulon. He is also a parachutist, having learnt that skill during his year of national service, and he recalls with pleasure the 20 free-fall jumps he has made. Neither those demanding activities nor the solitudes of circumnavigation have left any bleakness in his angular, handsome face. The light eyes are confidently direct beneath the thick brown hair, but their friendliness is free of the hard look that pride in self-sufficiency often brings.

When we met in a cool boat shed on the edge of Vannes, an old market town on the southern coast of Brittany, he didn't fit too well with the widespread impression of French yachtsmen as the pampered, overpaid darlings of the sport. Dressed in blue workman's overalls and ankle deep in the litter of preparation for the race, he was painting one of the twin hulls of *Crédit Agricole*.

'It is true that we are very lucky with the generous sponsorship in France, that it has given us a real advantage over yachtsmen in countries like the United States or Britain,' he said in English, first learnt at school and later made fluent on his travels as a diver. 'But nearly all the money goes on the

Jeantot: 'I calculate the percentages'

boats, on designing and building and maintaining them at competitive level, on insuring them, paying dock fees and meeting all the other expenses involved. When I entered the round-the-world race I had to sell my house in Brittany and practically everything else I owned. All the money I had earned from diving went to make up half of the $300,000 I needed to equip me with a boat that could win. I used to say that what I made below the sea I spent on top of it. The bank, Crédit Agricole, put up the other half of the money.

'This time Crédit Agricole are paying everything, but most of the four million francs they are investing is spent in the ways I have mentioned, to keep the yacht competitive over four years. They give me money to live on. I am not poor but I am not rich. Today is Saturday and tomorrow is Sunday and I am working for the boat. I am not in my armchair. In four or five years maybe skippers can come along on the day of the race, like Grand Prix drivers, and say "Okay guys, let's go."

'And yet perhaps we can never be stars like them. A Grand Prix lasts a couple of hours and if anything goes wrong the race is lost. You get out and leave the car. If you are sailing alone across an ocean and there is a bad problem you must make the repairs – not to win, just to survive.'

The painstaking thoroughness of Jeantot's dockside preparations for a voyage is already a legend. 'I approach it in the same way as I prepared to make a dive, trying to guard against everything that might go wrong. Fifty per cent of accidents in diving are caused by human mistakes. When you have been diving for a long time you forget about the risks and it becomes dangerous in those moments.'

Such a moment took Jeantot to the edge of death in 1979. He was working alone in low temperatures 120ft below the surface of the Straits of Magellan when the pump supplying the mixture of oxygen and helium he was breathing began to ice up. A message on his radio told the crew above he had nothing to breathe. 'They had to move fast – so they urinated on the equipment and thawed it enough to let them bring me to the surface. But there was no time for coming up in stages. I had to be hauled out and put in a decompression chamber.'

The calmness that is basic to his nature was no handicap in that crisis and it comes in useful on top of the water, too. Another of his important assets in the ordeal ahead will be fitness. His father, a bank official, but not with Crédit Agricole, encouraged him to be an all-round sportsman and his exertions at skiing, judo, karate, rowing and horse riding have helped to keep an athletic balance between his height (an inch or so under 6ft) and his weight of about 11st 11lb. At the time of our meeting he said that his training programme consisted mainly of jogging and smoking, but that the smoking was due to end abruptly when serious sailing began. He wanted his own performance to match the qualities he recognizes in the yacht designed for him by Gilles Ollier in Nantes and assembled in Vannes, where her original length of 21m was cut to the race limit of 60ft. The tiny cockpit – 6½ft wide by less than 5ft deep and just over 4ft high – gives his electronic aids more consideration than it grants him. As someone who cannot remember sleeping more than an hour at a stretch while sailing round the globe, he won't be put out unduly. He is happy to have the boat stripped of every unnecessary pound and delighted with the scientific tests he is sure have given her the aerodynamic qualities to outstrip the great majority in the race.

He acknowledges that the sprint across the Atlantic won't provide much opportunity for finding a dramatically original route. 'Any one of maybe 15 boats could present a major threat and each of us will know where the others are hour by hour.' With speeds of 28–30 knots within the capacity of so many, he is sure Weld's record will be dismembered. 'That record is old. This time the winner should cross in 14 or 15 days. I hope 14 for me and 15 for the next man.'

Philippe Jeantot may become rich in a country so in thrall to yacht racing that only four or five sports can have a greater hold on the public imagination. But it is easy to believe that he is more interested in having one beautiful boat and a few beautiful girlfriends than a pile of cash. 'Nobody who is a real sailor goes to sea for money', he insists. 'When you are sailing you are wet and cold, you don't sleep very well, you have not very good things to eat. Then you come back and tell everybody it was fantastic. Somehow you can't wait to be cold again, to be hungry, to be wet again.'

'Crédit Agricole' capsized on 7 June 1984. For 16 hours Jeantot's countryman Yvon Fauconnier stood by until rescue was on its way, before

resuming his course to victory. These unique photographs show the subsequent salvaging of 'Crédit Agricole'

A consistently popular feature in the *Observer Magazine* is called 'A Room of My Own'. Before the 1984 race the column went nautical and Ena Kendall talked to Rachael Hayward, who narrowly failed to be the only female finisher that year.

A CABIN OF HER OWN

Ena Kendall

Rachael Hayward, one of the few women competing in this year's race, hopes to reach Newport in about 28 days – certainly in time for 2 July, her 28th wedding anniversary. Unsponsored, she is competing in the amateur ideal 'to see if I can manage on my own', sailing *Loiwing*, a secondhand Sagitta 35 yacht.

We met when *Loiwing* was receiving her final sprucing at Ipswich Docks, where a skilled East Anglian team had been checking every last nut and bolt. Rachael knows the boat almost better than her own house because the Haywards have settled permanently in the United Kingdom only in the last five years – Roger Hayward's profession of civil engineer kept them abroad for the previous 23 – whereas they have owned *Loiwing* for nine years and sailed more than 20,000 miles in her. When Rachael made the decision to enter the race on the way back from the Azores last year, she contemplated sailing in a larger yacht, but decided to stick to her own craft, 35ft long and ten years old.

She is likely to spend a good deal of her time perched on the top step of the three leading from the cockpit down to the saloon, kettle and gas stove to hand on her right, the chart table on her left, and a view of the horizon ahead when she looks over the spray-board. There are two berths and she will use them both according to the tack the boat is on, so that she does not fall out. Just above the right-hand berth there is a glimpse of the lee cloth, a piece of sailcloth that can be slipped under the mattress and attached with rope to metal rings on the headboard to box her in for added safety.

In theory, she should not sleep for more than an hour at a time and is taking a battery of alarm clocks to ensure she doesn't. 'You have to look round the horizon every hour – if it's clear all round, you can snatch some sleep because it's supposed to take any approaching vessel an hour to hit you.' The boat will be on self-steering gear most of the time, but

Rachael Hayward aboard 'Loiwing'

148

the snag is that if the wind changes while she sleeps, it will take the boat in the wrong direction.

The chart table, with its nautical maps and reference books, is topped with a battery of equipment: a VHF radio telephone with a range of 40 miles, an echo sounder that tells the depth of water under the keel, a log for measuring distance and speed, a radar detector for use in fog and a satellite navigator, newly installed, that will keep her on course when fog or cloud makes celestial navigation impossible. She is not a practised navigator and usually her mathematically minded husband does it. 'But I take a sight with a sextant and use this excellent sight form that he has designed for me that says add or subtract and where to look things up.' She stows her buoyancy jacket, safety harness and distress flares in the space behind the chart table.

Rachael Hayward ran aground just six miles from the finish

The engine is boxed in behind the bottom step 'practically inaccessible for anything you want to do but never mind'. It is sealed before the start of the race, can only be used in case of trouble and then there is a time penalty. A few months ago she attended a one-day course on the marine diesel engine, learning how to service it and detect faults. 'Fortunately, I actually like machines.'

The sink has a salt-water pump so that she can use sea water for cooking vegetables, washing up and washing herself and so conserve the 35 gallons of fresh water she is carrying. She is taking as wide a variety of food as possible, including 'lots of onions, lots of garlic, potatoes and hard cabbages. Say it's a nice day and I'm not feeling too tired, I might cook a stew in my pressure cooker.' Her gas stove is gimballed which means it is on a swing so that it will

stay upright in a swell and there are bars to which pans and the kettle can be screwed. The food is stowed in a locker behind one berth, her clothes in the other. She is taking several changes of clothes, all packed individually in polythene bags so that they do not get wet before she puts them on. One of the new additions to *Loiwing* (named by its previous owner after a town on the Burma–China border) is a small gas heater on the wall. Rachael has sailed across the Atlantic twice before, though not alone, and harsh experience has taught her the wretchedness of being soaked and changing out of cold wet clothes in a cold wet cabin. Not that she is the sort to make a fuss about trifles like that: clear-minded and practical, she is a nimble figure in her Guernsey and denims, climbing expertly about the boat and making the voyage sound like a trip across the bay.

She was born in India in 1930, daughter of a commander of the Fifth Gurkha Rifles, and has two sons and a daughter, Amanda, who married last year and is now sailing round the world with her husband: they plan to meet her at Newport.

The Haywards sailed *Loiwing* the 7,500 miles from the United Kingdom to Dubai in 1976 and the two small fans were installed to cope with Red Sea weather. 'The Red Sea is horrible – we've been through it twice and next time I'm going through with air conditioning and stewards carrying glasses clinking with ice.' The first Red Sea passage saw an uninvited passenger, whose nibble marks are still visible on the right-hand berth's plastic cushions. The rat probably sneaked aboard at Ismailia when they were tied up to an old wooden jetty. 'We think it lived behind the chart table. We had nothing to kill it with so I crushed up some sleeping pills and mixed them with pâté, but it just went to sleep for a few days. We tried to knock it overboard – though I'd have been a bit worried if it had jumped – rats, you know, sinking ships and all that.' They endured it to Dubai where the municipal rat catcher caught it, and she never sails now without rat poison.

The whole time she is on deck she will be clipped on by her harness to lines called jackstays, an absolute rule: if she falls overboard no one will come and collect her. The North Atlantic in early June is unpredictable and she hopes not to encounter a hurricane, but the risks are less the weather than personal injury, spraining a wrist or breaking an ankle, or being run down in fog. She certainly has no hope of winning against the multihulled miracles of marine engineering built to break records, but she knows some of the other competitors and they will have a little contest within the race, testing seamanship and staying power. 'I think I'll probably feel lonely, particularly if the weather is wet and cold and beastly, and swear never to do it again.' She grinned – 'but you always do.'

When the flotilla of yachts gathered for the start of the 1984 OSTAR that doyen of singlehanders Phil Weld was absent. Surely it was not because this most youthful of navigators felt he was too old? Weld was asked to provide an explanation.

WHY I CHOSE NOT TO SAIL
Phil Weld

After *Moxie* and I won the 1980 OSTAR, let's admit it, normal boating for a time seemed anticlimactic. To restore my edge, I ordered a wing mast for *Rogue Wave*. Jan Gougeon trucked it to Manchester, Massachusetts, in mid-September 1981. Built 64ft tall of wood and epoxy weighing 750lb, it looked like a glider wing, paper-cutter slender. It promised to improve *Rogue's* performance to windward so that she could remain competitive for 1984. Since a rule revision had extended the overall length limit from 56 to 60ft, *Rogue Wave* was now eligible for the Observer race.

To break in what was then the world's tallest swivelling mast in the autumnal north-westers proved a challenge for me and my pre-OSTAR shipmate, Tom Perkins. In a 22-knot breeze, we could reach, 80 degrees off the true wind, under mast alone at 7 knots. We startled conventional craft by sailing past them with no sails at all as if we were under power. With sails up, we could tack in 85 degrees. Speed was greater on all points compared with the old cutter rig.

The roll-around-the-boom furling feature – a combination of bicycle chain and sprockets inside the base of the mast and a side-winding block on deck – had been intended as the answer to geriatric reefing. Alas, shortening the main by myself still proved to be exhausting. Yet to slab-reef 1,250 square feet of heavy Dacron, plus the heft of 11 full battens, daunted me.

At Walter Greene's Yarmouth, Maine, yard, we tried to make it easier. Credit the worst idea to me: a bicycle seat in the cockpit connected by sprocket and chain to two coffee-grinder winches, one for the main halyard and one for rotating the boom. A cycling handbook claimed foot-pedal power to be five times more efficient than cranking by hand. Not true, unless you can coast. The upstroke kills you. After two tries, we removed the contraption.

I had begun to regret my impulsive decision to give my 1980 race winner, *Moxie*, to the Navy. Incomprehensibly the Navy had sold her.

At Point à Pitre, Guadeloupe, for the finish in early December 1982 of the second running of the Route du Rhum, I was assailed by doubts. Young Frenchmen like Marc Pajot, the winner, with a 70ft aluminium wing mast on his 60ft catamaran, represented the solo-circuit future.

I loaned *Rogue* to Dick Newick for the Bermuda Multihull last June. She finished first. All July I brooded over 'boat divorce'. The Royal Western was prodding entries to release their slots on the 1984 roster unless they fully intended to start. Dick had entered *Rogue* in the Buzzard's Bay Regatta. With my acquiescence, he had invited Raymond Woodhead to fly from England to consider buying the boat. With Jan Gougeon, expert at trimming a wing mast, at the helm, *Rogue Wave* finished first in each of three races.

That Sunday night I couldn't sleep. I called Newick on Monday: 'Take her off the market. I'm picking her up for the Monhegan Race this weekend.' Thursday midnight a 35-knot north-easter caught us off Cape Porpoise. The wing mast has a triangular beak on its forward edge, waist high at its apex. Lines run port and starboard from the beak to blocks on the foredeck, then back to the cockpit. The padeye on the beak tore out as the wind gusted to 40. We had a real 'loose cannon on the deck'. Luckily Dave Shepard and Jim Deyo, Newick's two stalwarts, were able to tame the angrily rotating spar before it ripped out the tangs holding the shrouds aloft.

The weekend race around the Monhegan Islands buoy and back to Portland's harbour entrance proved a good light-air test of the rig. *Rogue* easily won the multihull division and passed all but three of the earlier-starting keel-boats. But throughout the race I pondered. Without drastic change there was no way one man could race *Rogue* competitively. Monday morning, as we powered through The Hussey, Mike Jacobs asked, 'Shall I check the chart?' 'No need,' said I, veering out of the channel to the west of the entrance bellbuoy to cut a corner for Portland Light, 'I know this trip by heart.'

At which point *Rogue*, proceeding homeward at 7 knots under diesel, lurched to a halt with a sickening thud. The tip of the daggerboard broke off on the one rock the chart shows in Hussey Sound. The mishap told me to head for the Vineyard, where Newick would sell her the next weekend to Raymond Woodhead, a charming Conradesque British adventurer, who had read of *Rogue* in my book, *Moxie*. He wanted to cruise the Indian Ocean from his home port, Abu Dhabi. A call to Plymouth relinquished my OSTAR slot.

In such a long race as OSTAR, 3,000 miles or more of turbulent ocean, the excitement of the winner crossing the line is usually succeeded by long waits for the next boats home and an inevitable sense of anti-climax. But 1984 was nail-bitingly different, as Trevor Grove discovered when he went out to Newport to cover the final days of the race for this book.

THE FINISH
Trevor Grove

He had sailed very hard. He had done his best. He knew his boat *Fleury Michon* very, very well. The small Frenchman with the rubbery grin and the damp gingery curls which didn't quite stop the TV lights bouncing off his bald crown was explaining how he had come to win the seventh Observer Singlehanded Transatlantic Race. Most of all, he said modestly, it was due to *'fortune de mer'*. Philippe Poupon had been lucky. In the last few days, as the four leading multihulls had raced almost bow-to-bow through Nantucket mists and fitful breezes, he had found 'a little bit of wind: *fortune de mer.'*

The throng of pressmen and well-wishers jostling around him were half inclined to believe this. No one had tipped Poupon before the race. He had a good long-distance track record and had sailed with Tabarly. He was a fit-looking 29. But back in Millbay Dock as the fleet made last-minute preparations for the race the crowds had had eyes only for Poupon's more celebrated countrymen – Pajot, Morvan, Tabarly and Jeantot – and for the two British hopefuls Peter Phillips and Jeff Houlgrave. *Fleury Michon* was a powerfully built trimaran, designed by John Shuttleworth. But she was slightly shorter than the real monsters and, besides, her sponsors didn't have quite the glamour of Colt Cars or Biotherm skin cream: they were France's second biggest purveyors of sausages. Yet a couple of hours ago Poupon and his boat had crossed the finishing line in the astonishing time of 16 days, 11 hours and 55 minutes, knocking a whole day and seven hours off the record set by Phil Weld four years earlier.

Delighted with his luck, Poupon left his own boat to be examined by a laconic US customs officer ('All I found on board was jes a li'l tiny bit a cheese') and elbowed through the TV crews to welcome the second yacht home. For a moment or two the hero of the hour was simply one of the crowd, a short man in a green and red anorak confident enough of his new stature as the fastest east–west Atlantic sailor in the world to risk temporary anonymity. He

Left: Champagne and roses for Philippe Poupon. Hours later he would be in tears when Fauconnier was declared the winner on corrected time

Destination Newport, Rhode Island: an idyllic landfall for transatlantic sailors

stood on tiptoe as Marc Pajot's colossal catamaran *Elf Aquitaine* was eased into her berth. It looked more like a tennis court with a mast on it than a yacht. Philippe and Marc met in the centre of the tennis court and posed for pictures.

Twelve hours later it was breakfast time on the morning of Tuesday, 19 June and Goat Island Marina was deserted. The rain was falling. The foghorn was still moaning at the mouth of Naragansett Bay. In the quayside press office elderly typewriters and Wang word processors (*Jesters* and *Elf Aquitaines* of the written word) sat exhausted side by side. From the door of the race committee headquarters a faint smell of last night's Gauloises and champagne dregs emerged to mingle with the whiff of ozone and diesel oil. And moored right alongside *Fleury Michon*, with its halyards ticking in the wind and rain dribbling down its shrouds, was *Umupro Jardin V*, which had been ninth across the line but which had by now been declared the official winner of the 1984 OSTAR on corrected time.

Yvon Fauconnier, *Umupro's* skipper, had spent 16 hours in mid-Atlantic standing by Philippe Jeantot's capsized catamaran *Crédit Agricole*. The race committee had decided, in accord with tradition and the rules of the sea, to discount the time Fauconnier had lost going to his compatriot's aid. Without the time allowance he had broken Phil Weld's 1980 record. With it he was, unambiguously, the victor of 1984. *'Fortune de mer.'*

Poupon didn't quite see it like that. On Monday night he had been at the centre of the stage, treading the dockside boards in salt-stained deck

Yvon Fauconnier greets his most loyal fans

shoes with a bouquet of roses in one arm, a bottle of Charles Heidsieck under the other and two dozen microphones under his nose. On Tuesday morning here he was exchanging broken English and despairing gesticulations with the Royal Western's race committee chairman Tom Pierce. 'But people will not understand why I am not the winner. I am the *first boat*.' And later: 'For me, this is the last time I am in this race. I used to like this race because it was simple. The winner was the winner. At sea you must take your fortune. Of course I would have stopped for Jeantot: but I would not have been the winner. Maybe in light winds in the future two sailors will "arrange" a rescue. . . .?' He looked sick and angry. 'Thank God', said an Englishman in earshot, 'the committee's decision benefited another Frenchman and not one of ours or an American. The French would never have entered this race again.' It was a sentiment repeated several hundred times that day.

Fauconnier came on to the dock looking spry and well breakfasted, in fresh white jeans and green sneakers. Another short, wiry man, smiling so much you could count the crow's feet at the corners of his eyes: there were nine deep wrinkles each side of his face, furrowing right down to his cheekbones. 'The sea was not organized', he said. 'Very short waves. Poupon? Yes, I have talked with him. We are still friends.'

A moment later the two men brushed against each other by accident. There was a sound like a low moan from the man who had won line honours but was not the winner. The luck of the sea can be fickle. . . . Later, at the press conference for the first

11 skippers home, an unnerving thing happened. The young man who has twice raced right round the world and who had just crossed one of its most treacherous oceans alone at record speed, one of the hard men of France's new breed of professional short-handed sailors, put his face behind his hands and wept.

Apart from Pajot, who put his arm round him, the other yachtsmen sat unmoved: granite-faced Tabarly; Peter Phillips, Britain's first man home, beaming good-naturedly; Warren Luhrs, whose blond good looks (a bearded version of Terence Stamp's Billy Budd) belied the efforts he must have made to bring a monohull boat in among the multi-hull leaders, breaking the record into the bargain.

But for the audience of relatives, journalists and TV crews from around the world, poor Poupon's misery was a moment of release as well as poignancy. For one thing, it was the cue for that enchanting old man of the sea, Phil Weld, to get up and say what everyone had been hoping someone would say: that this was a marvellous OSTAR because it had *two* winners instead of just one; and because the singlehanded brotherhood had shown that they were prepared to look after their own, not just churn on regardless towards the finish leaving coastguards and rescue helicopters to cope with the casualties. For another, this small but intense drama being played out in the banqueting room of the Sheraton Hotel signalled the end of a weekend of remarkable tension ashore as the race shaped up for the closest finish in the history of OSTAR.

For three days, while the narrow clapboard streets of Newport geared up for summer visitors

Poupon at the Goat Island press conference:
'The young man who had twice raced right round
the world and who had just crossed one of its most
treacherous oceans alone at record speed put his face
behind his hands and wept'

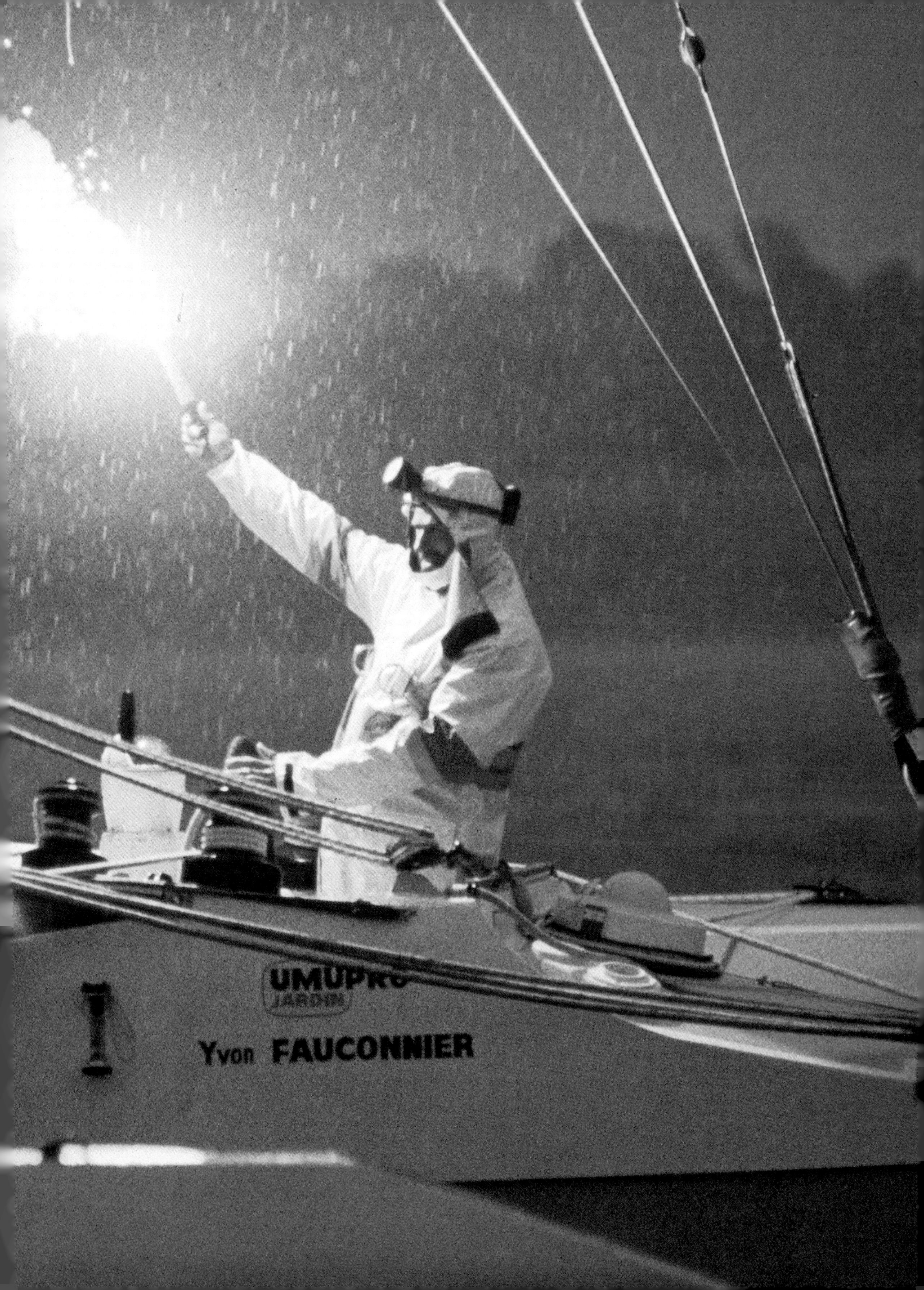
UMUPRO
JARDIN
Yvon FAUCONNIER

Preceding pages: Fauconnier and 'Umupro Jardin' show their winning flare. Above: Peter Phillips and family

and the great mansions out on Ocean Drive opened their shutters and mowed their prairie-sized lawns ready for the influx of house-guests, small planes had been flying off east beyond Nantucket, searching for sails. Satellite fixes from Argos were pored over twice a day. Numbered pins were inched forward on the big chart outside the race headquarters. It was like waiting for the finish of a marathon, uncertain about the last-minute changes of position after 26 miles of punishing running – with the difference that here was a fleet of boats which had followed dozens of different courses across 3,000 miles of ocean, out of sight of each other, largely out of touch with land, and always prey to Poupon's *'fortune de mer'*.

Over the weekend the rich buzz of Devonian accents had transformed the Goat Island bar into a West Country pub on a Saturday night. Out there somewhere beyond the Brenton Tower was Peter Phillips, former Exeter policeman and skipper of another Shuttleworth-designed trimaran, *Travacrest Seaway*. Phillips had been leading the pack for

a whole nail-biting week. In the bar, fortified by cups of tea and cigarettes, were his wife Joan, his twin 19-year-old daughters and one of his two sons (not the one who had somewhat thoughtlessly planned to get married on the day of the start and had had to advance the wedding date!).

Gathered round Joan and the family were some of the volunteer team who had built Peter's boat for him in a hired shed in Honiton in 26 weeks of dedicated unpaid labour, all for about the same cost as *Elf Aquitaine*'s wing mast. The team had included a plumber, an out-of-work chef, a man from the Electricity Board, two policemen, a photocopier engineer and kids from the local approved school.

Not much is written about the wives of men like Peter Phillips. How do they put up with it? Married singlehanders leave singlehanded spouses at home for months every year. Why do they endure it? Joan, no sailor herself, provides some of the answers as well-wishers crowd round her teacup-laden table. She is funny about the occasions when she's had to

Marc Pajot, second man home, shows little sign of strain as he is greeted in Newport

Philippe Jeantot: not much to smile at

Warren Luhrs: magical monohuller

give over the washing machine to Genoa sheets rather than the other kind; she describes a home that's a kind of glorified sail-loft; she becomes nostalgic about the way Peter would come to bed with a clipboard in case he should have a new thought about the race preparations in the middle of the night. She put up with it, she says, because she's a policeman's wife and because she would never want to divorce him from his sailing. By the time she'd met him – at the age of 15, at a fairground – he was already dedicated to boats. He had started with a punt called *Pancake*. . . .

The Devon lads ordered Budweisers. Someone from *The Observer* office came in with news. Early on Father's Day (Sunday, 17 June) an aeroplane had spotted *Fleury Michon* at 41° 22′ N, 66° 10′ W with her spinnaker up but 'dead in the water'. *Elf Aquitaine* had some wind and was reaching at 4–5 knots. There was no sign of *Travacrest*. . . .

'Oh, I wish I could get out there and give him a kick', said Joan. If only he hadn't installed that extra-heavy bilge pump. If only his waterlogged radio didn't weigh so much. Why didn't he just chuck it overboard?

'Hello *Travacrest Seaway*. Hello *Travacrest Seaway*. This is Observer Race Control. Do you read me? Over.' As the Argos satellite readings showed the leaders coming into range on Monday the VHF sets crackled and roared into the void. Unknown to patient Joan and her supporters, Peter's light air Genoa, vital for the freakish conditions of the last few miles, had blown out – 'split from luff to leach', said Peter later. Worse, he'd fallen overboard, fortunately in light winds so he had been able to scramble aboard again. He had watched Poupon overtake him.

By six o'clock on Monday evening, a sea-change occurred at the Goat Island Marina. Suddenly windowless vans arrived, parked, and started cranking up enormous masts with antennae at their tips, taller than the masts of the Onion Patch ocean racers moored beside them. French broke out. There were Frenchmen in oilskins, Frenchmen waving ENG cameras, Frenchmen talking into tape

Victory salute: by the man declared the winner though he didn't come in first

Victory salute: by the man who broke the tape, broke the record — and then broke down

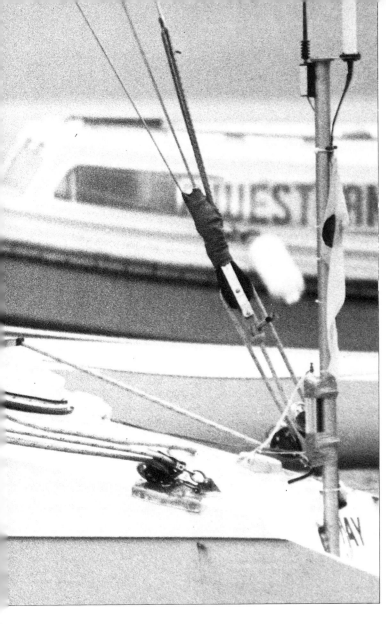

recorders. Two Newport cops with handcuffs hanked onto their belts took up station. The Royal Western contingent put on their yachting caps. It began at last to feel as though a great international sporting event was about to occur; marine engines throbbed into life as the spectator fleet set off, heading for the Brenton Tower.

'Une voile,' said the Frenchman from the Argos company, pointing off the starboard bow. 'Une voile.' Now everyone could see it: a thin grey shadow that was rapidly becoming a thick grey shadow and growing a trio of bouncing hulls at its base. It had to be Poupon. The US coastguard launch fired pink flares and Very lights as Fleury Michon stormed out of the twilight at 15 knots, zipped past the Brenton Tower with Poupon doing a boxer's salute and abruptly decelerated to let the Royal Western commodore, Johnny Dacre, jump aboard for the post-race inspection. Just then 'une voile!' again from the eagle-eyed Argos man: it was Elf Aquitaine, the flying tennis court with the enormous wing mast which had caused such head-shaking back in Plymouth. Marc Pajot was just 23 minutes behind Philippe Poupon.

Later that evening Tabarly's ungainly hydro-foiler Paul Ricard, more like a seaplane than a yacht, ghosted into harbour. Under the glare of the TV lighting the father of French yachting scraped a hand through the stubble on his chin and made it first, second and third for France, even before Fauconnier arrived to multiply la Gloire by four.

It was all happening so quickly. The dockside crowds tramped this way and that as the great tired multihulls (and later Luhrs's mono, Thursday's Child) crept in out of the night with their sails down and under tow, each yacht leaving a broken record in her wake. Long after their skippers had gone off to enjoy a decent sleep in a real bed, people stayed and stared, and stared.

Out there somewhere the rest of the fleet still flogged westwards, the little boats and the amateur sailors – including brave Rachael Hayward, by this time the only woman left in the race. But on the quay Peter Phillips hid his disappointment and hugged Joan and the kids and held on to a pint mug of beer. He looked like a jovial, half-shaven Captain Ahab: his razor had given out. 'I could stand here and talk all night', he said to the throng, having not been able to get through on his radio since leaving the Channel. While he told them how he had lived mainly on fruit and chocolate and tins of beans, listening to James Last and Neil Diamond tapes for relaxation, Joan's eyes never left his face.

'Will you tell him not to do it again, Joan?'

'Oh no, I wouldn't do that. Stop him sailing? It would be like taking a dummy away from a baby.'

Some baby.

'Fleury Michon' stormed out of the twilight at 15 knots on the evening of 18 June, having travelled 3,205 miles at an average speed of 8.09 knots

The sight Newport never saw: Florence Arthaud and 'Biotherm' gave up long before the finish, leaving only Rachael Hayward to keep the distaff flying – and she ran aground just miles from the finish

OTHERM II

'Elf Aquitaine' before the start; the flying tennis court roared into Newport just 23 minutes behind 'Fleury Michon'. Pajot's success with this revolutionary rig was a remarkable achievement. Overleaf: 'L'Aiglon' and 'Paul Ricard'

*Yvon Fauconnier on course for Newport
and the victor's laurels —
though he didn't know it at the time*

UMUPRO JARDIN V

After 3,000 miles or so the shock of making human contact again is considerable – though Fauconnier seemed pleased enough to see the journalists and TV crews lining the quayside. Drops of rain and spray splatter the camera lens

This was supposed to be the OSTAR in which
the multihullers finally proved that more traditional
craft could no longer compete. Warren Luhrs
came in ninth (tenth after the Fauconnier decision)
and proved them wrong. Here is 'Thursday's
Child' with a conventional crew aboard

'Travacrest Seaway' shows her heels. If the nation which invented the Observer Singlehanded Transatlantic Race is to win it again, it will be with a boat as purposefully designed as this one and with a skipper as dedicated as Peter Phillips

The first consideration when victualling for OSTAR must be nourishment for at least 15 and possibly 50 days. Against this must be balanced the need to keep weight to a minimum. Many yachtsmen also think it is important to keep in good psychological shape by eating well, if not luxuriously. It is not as simple as one might imagine . . .

FOOD FOR FUEL

Libby Purves

In 1960 *The Observer*'s correspondent at the start recorded that 'the strawberries went aboard Blondie Hasler's boat yesterday afternoon. This morning the last of the salads were put aboard. . . .' Lt.-Col. Hasler also shipped supplies of wheat, which he ground up himself in a coffee-mill and mixed with sea water to make loaves. 'If I arrive last,' he said on the way, 'it will be because baking bread and eating it has occupied all my attention.'

Stores are taken on board 'Livery Dole', Peter Phillips's craft in the 1980 race

Francis Chichester, meanwhile, was logging robust meals of fried egg and potato; private feasts of chocolate, and one 'tea of kippers and stout' washed down with whisky-and-lime. Apart from anything else, such tastes betoken an enviable mastery over seasickness.

Contrary to much popular belief, it is perfectly possible, when stowing a boat for one person for up to 50 days at sea, to ensure that this one person eats both appetizingly and wholesomely. Before the 1970s explosion of convenience foods for yachtsmen, Hasler, Tabarly, Richey and others established the principle of using traditional, unrefined foods – rice, spaghetti, dried fruit and dried or salted meat (in 1968 Michael Richey took an entire dried haunch of Norwegian sheep). One of *Jester*'s lists even includes the unlikely luxury 'sea salt – two packets', although one would have thought there would be plenty of that commodity to be harvested by scraping the seams of the sails. Hard vegetables, such as onions and cabbage, were popular; perhaps some remembered the great H. W. Tilman's dictum 'never board a ship without an onion'.

However, not all competitors have been such bons viveurs as the early singlehanded racers. Two considerations arise: firstly, you may not wish to cook anything at all; secondly, you may need to keep cargo weight down. The race has furthered several developments for hungry non-cookers: the present crop of excellent boil-in-foil casseroles is one example, another is the curious 'hot can' system, where a chemical reaction heats the food inside the very tin. This also saves washing up and fuel. Indeed, fuel itself takes up space and weight allowances; one past competitor, after he had lost a tankful of paraffin, ended up trying to eat a revolting cereal of rice powdered up with a mallet and mixed with longlife milk.

As for weight-saving, the most extreme example must be that of David Blagden, skipper of the

Fruit and vegetable merchant Alec Rose on 'Lively Lady' in 1964

smallest boat ever in the race, the 18ft *Willing Griffin*, which crossed in 1972 taking 52 days. The committee, he wrote, despite the stringent regulations on equipment, 'didn't stipulate that I had to have a pleasant and varied diet'. So he saved every ounce, calculating calorific output per gram and minimum bulk and waste; concluding that the best thing was to pack one Royal Marine Arctic One-Day Ration Pack for every *two* days of the voyage. One sailor needs less than one cold Marine, apparently. Even so, Blagden disliked some of the spreads and meat products so much that he never ate them. One cannot wonder. In all the history of gastronomy, has anyone invented a less appealing title for a meal than 'mutton granules'? Blagden also heroically confined himself to two pints of water a day, much of which went in reconstituting mutton granules and the like.

With the advent of the ultra-lightweight multihulls, even skippers of 60-footers began to find that they shared Blagden's problem of cargo weight. To this, many hard racers added an unwillingness to spare sailing energy on cooking duties; and perhaps also a lack of interest. With the expected crossing times down to just over a fortnight, food took on a lower priority than in the six-week era.

However it came about, Peter Phillips's 1984 list (reproduced overleaf) would bring a shudder to the more old-fashioned spirits of the 1960s. His predilection for cheese cheers up the otherwise dully tinned diet; and it is reassuring to see that a British ship, however racy, does not deny itself tea, Bovril, or cocoa; nonetheless it does not read like the ingredients of a fortnight's gastronomic cruise.

One might expect a French multihuller to eat a little better; but Marc Pajot's complete list from *Elf Aquitaine II* strikes horror even deeper into the gourmet soul. Far from enjoying the fine French saucissons and bottles of Côtes du Rhône shipped by Hasler and Richey, Pajot took, in 1984:

'Longlife bread; protein paste of various flavours; yoghurt; fresh fruit; no alcohol, no tea, coffee, milk, or sweets. Mineral water in plastic bottles.'

And that, we were assured, was the lot.

Here are four lists of provisions, illustrating the four approaches you can take: Clare Francis's comfortable 'cruising' supplies aboard the roomy *Robertson's Golly* in 1976; Peter Phillips's stores aboard *Travacrest Seaway* in 1984; Michael Richey's supplies for 58 days in 1972; and David Blagden's one-day Marine ration packs, spread over two days' sailing each.

Clare Francis

General provisions

6 jars Robertson's marmalade
6 jars Robertson's jam
2 jars Robertson's mincemeat
4 large packets All Bran
4 large packets Prewitt's Muesli
4 packets Jordan's Original Crunchy Cereal
2 packets porridge oats
2lb white flour
6lb Felin Geri wholemeal flour
3lb granary breadmeal flour
10oz dried yeast
22 packets savoury rice
3 packets spaghetti
4 packets egg noodles
10 cartons Long Life milk
2 large tins dried milk
1 jar coffee
144 tea bags
1 large tin Ovaltine
2 bottles lime juice
2 bottles lemon and lime juice
2 bottles concentrated apple juice
2 packets brown sugar
1 large can vegetable oil
1 bottle wine vinegar
4 cartons Cup-a-Soup
8 packets dried soup
1 bottle tomato sauce
8 small tins tomato purée
1 jar mustard
1 bottle Worcestershire sauce
6 jars pickled onions
2 jars honey
1 large bag raisins
1 large bag nuts
6 packets Viota crumble mix
2 packets Viota pastry mix
6 sauce mixes (cheese, white, parsley)
6 packets dried prawn curry
4 pizza mixes
2 packets instant mashed potato
2 packets dried peas
3 packets vegetable stock cubes
1 parmesan cheese
1 jar Marmite
1 tin custard powder
4 packets dates
10 packets oatcakes

3 fruit cakes
11 packets sweet biscuits
8 packets savoury biscuits
8 bars chocolate
8 pots fish paste
6 tins sardines
6 tins salmon
Herbs, pepper, salt

Tinned provisions

26 grapefruit/orange juice
10 soup
4 Robertson's new potatoes
4 Robertson's carrots
6 sweet corn
5 tomatoes
3 green beans
5 broad beans
3 baked beans
4 mushrooms
2 spinach
2 stuffed peppers
4 artichoke hearts
8 asparagus tips
20 Robertson's peaches
20 Robertson's plums
10 Robertson's fruit pie fillings
10 Robertson's cherries
10 gooseberries
10 pears
10 mandarin oranges
5 prunes
5 blackberries
6 chestnuts (*marrons*)
8 cream
8 custard

Fresh provisions

4 pints milk
3 cartons yoghurt
12 loaves bread
1½lb butter
5 cartons vegetable margarine
10 dozen eggs
5lb cheese
5lb potatoes
15 large onions
4lb carrots
1 cabbage
4 trays tomatoes
1 lettuce
2 cucumbers
8 pears
10 grapefruits
15 oranges
4 bunches bananas
20 apples
15 gallons fresh water

Francis Chichester: his meals of fried eggs and potato, kippers and stout defied seasickness

 ## Peter Phillips

Hot can prepared meals (self-heating)
Tinned meat
Packet soups
Oxo, Bovril
Tea, coffee, drinking chocolate, squash
Steak and kidney pudding, tinned
Irish stew
Rice pudding, tinned
Tinned fish
Longlife milk
2½ dozen eggs
Margarine
Nuts, chocolate, sweets, Mars bars
3lb cheese
Cheese spreads of all flavours
14 loaves bread, 24 rolls
Crackers

Fruit:
    14 oranges
    14 apples
    10 green bananas
    1 pineapple
Tomatoes
Cucumbers
No alcohol (this is a dry ship, except for one bottle
    of whisky put on board by Chay Blyth)

 ## Michael Richey

'House dried' Burgundy ham, from which pieces
    were cut as required
40 onions
6 cloves garlic
48 oranges
18 plastic lemons
48 apples
6 tins olive oil
6 packets figs
6 packets nuts
6 packets dates
1 packet sunflower seed
4 tins ships' biscuits (Carr's) (2 tins left)
7lb muesli (2lb left)
12 packets Gemma spaghetti imported from Italy
    ('wheat germ put back') (6 left)
3 boxes Complan
1 large Cheddar cheese
10lb unpolished rice (7lb left)
8 dozen eggs, rubbed with lard
6lb tinned butter (4lb left)
6 packets parmesan cheese ⎫   for
6 tubes promodoso sauce ⎭   spaghetti
8 tins powdered milk (3 left)
6lb coffee (2lb left)
1½lb tea (1½lb left)
6lb soft brown sugar (5lb left)
6 jars honey (2 jars left)
2lb marmalade (1lb left)
25 bouillon cubes
2 packets sea salt
24 packets Barbados chocolate
200 pints water (20 pints left)
7 gallons wine   ⎫
6 bottles whisky   ⎪   all finished in
1 bottle champagne   ⎬   first month
1 bottle brandy   ⎭

David Blagden

Menu A

Breakfast:
    Rolled oats with milk and sugar
    Cocoa
Snack:
    Biscuits
    Meat spread
    Dextrosol lime flavour
    Chocolate
    Confectionery bar
    Nuts and raisins
Drinks:
    Coffee, tea, Bovril
Main meal:
    Onion soup
    Beef granules
    Mashed potatoes
    Mixed vegetables
    Apple flakes

Menu B

Breakfast:
    Rolled oats with milk and sugar
    Cocoa
Snack:
    Biscuits
    Chicken spread
    Dextrosol orange flavour
    Chocolate
    Confectionery bar
    Nuts and raisins
Drinks:
    Coffee, tea, Bovril
Main meal:
    Mock turtle soup
    Curried beef granules
    Pre-cooked rice
    Carrots
    Apple and bilberry flakes

Menu C

Breakfast:
    Rolled oats with milk and sugar
    Cocoa
Snack:
    Biscuits
    Cheese
    Dextrosol lemon flavour
    Chocolate
    Confectionery bar
    Nuts and raisins
Drinks:
    Coffee, tea, Bovril
Main meal:
    Oxtail soup
    Mutton granules
    Mashed potatoes
    Peas
    Apple flakes

Menu D

Breakfast:
    Rolled oats with milk and sugar
    Cocoa
Snack:
    Biscuits
    Chicken and ham spread
    Dextrosol lime flavour
    Chocolate
    Confectionery bar
    Nuts and raisins
Drinks:
    Coffee, tea, Bovril
Main meal:
    Oxtail soup
    Chicken supreme
    Pre-cooked rice
    Mixed vegetables
    Apple and bilberry flakes

Right: 'Three Cheers', skippered by Tom Follett in 1972. She disappeared in the 1976 OSTAR

There have been major and minor changes in the rules and conditions of entry in the 25 years since the first Observer Singlehanded Transatlantic Race. To illustrate these, rules and entry forms for the first race, in 1960, and the latest, in 1984, are given on the pages that follow.

RULES AND CONDITIONS OF ENTRY 1960

ORGANIZATION

1. The Royal Western Yacht Club of England will be the organizing Club, will deal with all entries and will Start the race.

   The Slocum Society have very kindly agreed to be responsible for the finishing arrangements.

OBJECT

2. The race is intended to be a sporting event, and to encourage the development of suitable boats, gear, supplies and technique for singlehanded ocean crossings under sail.

AWARDS

3. A trophy will be presented by the Organizers to the competitor adjudged to be the winner, to be retained by him as his permanent possession. Other subsidiary prizes will be awarded, as decided by the Organizers.

DATE

4. The start will be from Plymouth, England, at 10 am BST on Saturday, 11 June 1960.

COURSE

5. By any route to the finishing line off Ambrose Light Vessel, in the approaches to New York Harbour. Great Circle distances are approximately as follows: Total distance 3,000 nautical miles; minimum ocean crossing (Ireland to Newfoundland) 1,700 nautical miles.

ENTRIES

6. An entry will consist of a sailing boat (hereafter called 'the yacht') plus a named crew of one person only ('the crew'). The crew must be over 21 years of age, but need not be the owner of the yacht, and may be man or woman, amateur or professional.

7. Entries will be made under the nationality of the crew. The yacht need not have been designed or built in that country.

8. Entries may be sponsored and/or financed by another person, body or organization.

9. Each intending entrant should apply in writing to The Secretary, Royal Western Yacht Club of England, enclosing cheque or money order for his entrance fee (Rules 10 and 11), made payable to the Secretary, Royal Western Yacht Club.

ENTRANCE FEES

10. For applications reaching the Club on or before **Friday, 15 May 1960**, the entrance fees will be £15 0s. 0d. This will be refunded to the entrant after he has officially started in the race, and has arrived singlehanded at any port over 100 miles from the start. Otherwise it will be retained.

11. Late entries may be accepted up to and including Saturday, 4 June 1960, but must be accompanied by an entrance fee of £25 0s. 0d. which will not be refunded.

EVIDENCE OF QUALIFICATION

12. An entrant must have completed a singlehanded qualifying cruise of a nature to satisfy the organizing committee, or, alternatively, must furnish a Certificate of Competence. This will be accepted in lieu of Evidence of Qualification, provided that it is signed by a Flag Officer of an established Yacht Club or other competent body

known and approved by the Organizers. The Certificate must say of the competitor that he/she 'is in my opinion competent to undertake a long singlehanded ocean passage in a small yacht'.

PASSPORT AND VISA

13.   Entrants will be required to furnish themselves with, and to produce before the race, valid documents for entry into the USA.

ELIGIBILITY OF YACHTS

14.   Yachts of any size or type may enter, subject to the decision of the Organizers. (It is not their desire to exclude yachts solely on grounds of unconventional type or design.) There will be no handicapping.

15.   No means of propulsion may be employed other than the force of the wind, the man-power of the crew, or both.

16.   An internal combustion engine, which must be incapable of being used to propel the yacht, may be used to generate electricity for lighting or radio, but NOT for operating self-steering gear, nor for handling sails or ground tackle. This engine may be the yacht's auxiliary engine, provided that the propeller has been removed, or the shaft sealed before the start.

Where this is impracticable, and the crew wishes to retain his propeller in situ, this will be allowed, provided that he only carries sufficient fuel for battery charging and that he signs a declaration at the finish to the effect that the engine has not been used for other purposes except that it may be used for entering and leaving harbour, instead of being towed, within the limits set out in Paragraph 22.

INSPECTION

17.   Each yacht will be open to inspection by the Organizers, and by other entrants, at a specified time before the start, and again immediately after the finish.

18.   **Condition Inspection.** Although no stipulations (except as stated elsewhere in the rules) will be made as to design, construction, rig, or equipment of yachts, each yacht will be required to pass a 'Condition Inspection', after she is afloat, and equipped with all essential sailing equipment for the race. The inspection may be carried out by any practising Marine Surveyor, at the entrant's expense, not earlier than 15 March 1960. Alternatively, it may be carried out at the Organizers' expense at Plymouth, by a Surveyor to be appointed by the Organizers, not earlier than 1 June 1960. The results of such inspection will be recorded in the following form:

'I/We hereby certify that I/we have today inspected the yacht .... (name, port, number, etc.)........... lying afloat at ...., rigged and equipped with all essential sailing equipment (including navigational equipment) which .... (name of entrant) proposes to carry and use in the Singlehanded Atlantic Race. Insofar as it was possible to inspect them, I/we consider that the hull, decks, spars, rigging, sails, ground tackle, fittings and sailing equipment appeared to be in a good and serviceable condition, except for the following items .... (delete if necessary).' This certificate must reach the Organizers not later than 10 am on Thursday, 9 June 1960. If any item has failed to pass the inspection, the crew will be responsible for obtaining a further certificate, from the Organizers' Surveyor at Plymouth, that the items have been satisfactorily repaired or replaced. Failure to satisfy this rule will result in disqualification before the start.

SAFETY EQUIPMENT

19.   The crew will be required to carry certain safety equipment, as listed below, throughout the race, and for maintaining it in serviceable condition. It is hoped that certain of these articles may be available on loan.

Inflatable Life Raft
Radar Reflector
Portable Loud Hailer
Foghorn
Daylight Distress Signals and Marker Dye
Flares and Pyrotechnic Distress Signals.

CONDUCT OF RACE

20.   **Late Starters.** An entrant who fails to be ready for the start may arrange with the Organizers to be allowed to start at any time up to two weeks after the start, by arrangement with the Organizers, but will thereafter be regarded as having started at the official time.

OUTSIDE ASSISTANCE

21.   No physical contact, except for the passing of written messages, may be made with other ships or boats at sea, and no stores to be received from any other ship during the race. They may, however, be asked for advice or information, and to report the yacht's position and condition.

22.   During the race, a yacht may put in anywhere, and anchor or moor for any purpose. She may be towed for a distance not exceeding two miles into, and for a distance not exceeding two miles out of, any such harbour or anchorage, provided that the total result of such towage can be shown not to have advanced the yacht towards the finish. When actually moored or anchored, other people may

come aboard, stores or equipment may be embarked, and repairs effected.

RESPONSIBILITY

23. Yachts must be fully independent, and capable of carrying out their own emergency repairs at sea. Crews have no right to expect or demand rescue operations to be launched on their behalf.

24. Full responsibility for any mishap will rest with the owner or crew under ordinary processes of law. The Organizers do not accept any responsibility towards the entrants, nor towards third parties with whom the entrants may become involved.

RECOGNITION

25. A distinguishing number should at all times be prominently displayed on the yacht's hull and sails.

DECLARATION

26. Immediately after finishing, each crew will be required to sign a declaration that he has sailed the race in accordance with all published rules, or, if any rule has been broken, to give a full account of the circumstances, establishing to what, if any, extent the yacht's progress towards the finish was helped by the breach in question.

FINISHERS

27. In order to qualify as a finisher, a yacht must finish not later than 11 September 1960.

AUTHORITY

28. These rules, dated 31 March 1960, are published by the Royal Western Yacht Club of England, who reserve the right to amend, or add to, the rules at any time up to the start of the race, such amendments being immediately promulgated to all entrants who have been provisionally accepted. Additional instructions will, in any case, be issued by the Organizers to cover details of the starting and finishing arrangements.

ROYAL WESTERN YACHT CLUB OF ENGLAND SINGLEHANDED TRANSATLANTIC RACE, 1960

Form of Entry

To: The Secretary, Royal Western Yacht Club of England, Plymouth.

Name of Yacht....................Rig..
Registered Number........Flag of Registry or nationality........
Tons T.M..
Length.............Beam..............Draught ....
Sail Number (which will be used during the race).................

Owner ....
Address ....
Crew's Name..
Crew's Address..
    I (name of Crew)....................................DECLARE that I am over the age of 21 years and that I wish to enter the above yacht for the Singlehanded Transatlantic Race and in the event of my Entry being accepted I agree (a) that the sponsors and organizers of the Race shall have no liability either to me or my estate for any accident or loss arising consequent upon my entry and participation in the said Race and (b) to indemnify the sponsors and organizers of the Race in respect of any liability or loss whatsoever and howsoever arising consequent upon my entry and participation in the said Race whether such liability or loss shall be incurred in respect of myself, the yacht, third parties, another entrant in the said Race or in any other respect.

    I accept the jurisdiction of the Organizers on all matters to do with the eligibility and disqualification.

    I accept the jurisdiction of the Organizers on all matters to do with trophies and awards.

    I agree to assist the Organizers by doing all I can to send back position and condition reports during the course of the Race (this may involve the use of radio transmission assuming that the necessary equipment is available).

    I enclose herewith the sum of ..... being my Entrance Fee.

Signed ....

Witness ....
Address of Witness...
    ....
Occupation of Witness..
Date...

Right: Rule changes have affected the maximum length of OSTAR *entries, but little else about their design. This is Tabarly watching his 67ft trimaran 'Pen Duick IV' being built in February 1968*

RULES AND CONDITIONS OF ENTRY 1984

(All times are GMT unless otherwise stated)

1. ORGANIZATION

The Race will be organized by the Royal Western Yacht Club of England.

2. OBJECT

The Race is intended to be a sporting event, and to encourage the development of suitable boats, gear, supplies and technique for shorthanded ocean crossings under sail.

3. PRIZES

Prizes will be awarded to the first yacht to finish, regardless of type or class, and to the first monohulled and first multihulled yachts in each class except that no yacht may win more than one main prize.

Prizes will also be awarded to the second and third yachts in each class regardless of type.

All yachts finishing will be awarded a memento.

4. DATE

The start will be from Plymouth, England, at 1200 BST on Saturday, 2 June 1984.

5. COURSE

The course will be from Plymouth to the finishing line off Newport Rhode Island by any route leaving NANTUCKET ISLAND to Starboard.

6. ENTRIES

6.1   Entries will be limited to 80 competitors plus a further 20 at the discretion of and by invitation from the Committee.

A skipper may reserve a place in the race by completing the attached Entry Form and sending it together with an entry fee of £300 to the Secretary of the Royal Western Yacht Club. This entry fee is not refundable.

6.2   Entries will be made under the nationality of the crew. The yacht need not have been designed or built in that country.

6.3   If requested by the owner for bona fide reasons, and approved by the Race Committee, the crew may be replaced by another properly qualified person (Rule 7.2) until 24 hours before the start. From this time on the crew must not be changed.

6.4   Entries may be sponsored and/or financed by another person, body or organization. The RWYC is not averse to the sponsoring of entries and is indeed glad of the help that has been given to the competitors in the previous Races, which undoubtedly added to the interest in them. Nevertheless they are concerned that this Race should remain a sporting event and reserve the right to refuse an entry if it appears that the primary object of it is to promote a commercial project not connected with the object of the Race.

In particular a Yacht owned or sponsored wholly or partly by a group or organization may not display any advertising except by means of her name and/or a Logo or emblem. The lettering of the name must not exceed $\frac{1}{3}$ of the yacht's freeboard in height nor $\frac{1}{3}$ of the yacht's overall length in length and may be displayed only once on each side. Any logo must not exceed the height and width of the largest letter of the yacht's name. There may be only one such logo or emblem on each side of the hull and on each side of each sail. The name must not contain more than 20 letters, any space between two words counting as one letter. The Committee reserves the right to reject a name which they consider to be offensive or distasteful and will give an advanced ruling on request.

Where publicity for a yacht's sponsors is obtained by an entry in the race, for example by the name of the yacht, an additional 'sponsored entry fee' of £300 will be payable.

Where more than one yacht bears the same name they must be identified by the addition of a name rather than a number and this must be agreed by the Committee, e.g. SPONSOR LADY and SPONSOR ENTERPRISE rather than SPONSOR I and SPONSOR II.

6.5   Entries should be made so as to reach the Secretary, RWYC of E, by 14 April 1984. The applications should include:

(a) An entry form completed. (Where the qualifying cruise has yet to be completed the details called for in Rule 8 may be submitted later but see Rule 6.)

(b) Cheque or money order for entry fee (Rule 6.1). (Cheques from overseas should be drawn on a London Bank.)

Entries will be accepted in the order of a correctly completed Entry Form and Entry Fee being received at the Royal Western Yacht Club. When the limit of entries has been reached further applicants will be placed on a waiting list, if they so desire, up to the closing date for entries to be received. No further entries will be accepted after this date.

6.6 The qualifying cruise (Rule 7.2) must have been successfully completed before 31 March 1984.

6.7 An applicant whose entry is not accepted by the Committee will be informed of the reason as soon as possible and his entry fee returned.

6.8 An applicant whose application is approved by the Committee will be accepted as a provisional entry.

6.9 Every provisional entry must arrive in Plymouth by 2000, Saturday 26 May. His yacht must be ready in all respects for inspection am Monday 28 May. Any yacht arriving late will be subject to a time penalty of 25 per cent of the time late. This will be added to the yacht's elapsed time.

6.10 The Committee will be ready to start inspecting any entries who desire it on Saturday 26 May.

6.11 Any entry who has not been accepted by 1200 on Friday 1 June will be subject to a time penalty or a delayed start.

6.12 Entries will close at 2359 on 14 April 1984.

6.13 The name of a yacht may not be changed after the closing date for entries.

7. ELIGIBILITY OF YACHTS AND CREWS

7.1 The race is open to seaworthy cruising or racing yachts of any size, type or nationality, provided that the overall length is not less than 25ft (7.62m) nor more than 60ft (18.29m). The Race Committee reserves the right to exclude any yacht which it regards as unseaworthy or a yacht with inadequate equipment, but unorthodox and multi-hulled yachts are admissible, with the exception of PROAS, which are specifically excluded.

7.2 The entrant must fill in on the entry form details of his/her Ocean Racing and/or Offshore Cruising experience. Entrants must show that they have sailed at least 500 miles as skipper or 1,000 miles as crew before their qualifying cruises described below. Before the closing date for qualifying the entrant must have completed a singlehanded qualifying cruise of not less than 500 miles in the open sea without anchoring or putting into port. The 500 miles must be measured in straight lines joining not more than four points on his cruise track. The cruise must be made in the yacht he/she intends to enter in the race. He may not be escorted at any stage by any other vessel. In addition, each yacht must have done a cruise of at least 1,000 miles with the prospective entrant on board but not necessarily by himself. This cruise must reach a distance of at least 300 miles from its starting point and must be made in the open sea. It may however include any number of stopping places.

7.3 In the event of any entrant being found to have made a false statement his entry will be refused and his entry fee forfeit.

8. MONOHULLS AND MULTIHULLS

In order to be classed as a monohull, a boat must have a single rigid hull (as opposed to two or more hulls joined rigidly together). If the Committee considers that a design has been expressly intended to bring into the Monohull class a boat that has some characteristics of a multihull, it may arbitrarily classify her as a multihull. Designers who are working on 'Hybrids' of this sort are invited to submit their early sketch designs to the Committee for a ruling.

9. CLASSES

CLASS I   Over 45ft (13.72m) to 60ft (18.29m)
      II   Over 40ft (12.19m) to 45ft (13.72m)
     III   Over 35ft (10.67m) to 40ft (12.19m)
     IV   Over 30ft (9.42m) to 35ft (10.67m)
     V   Over 25ft (7.62m) to 30ft (9.14m)

Example: A yacht measuring exactly 40ft will be Class III.

The upper limits of each class are defined solely by length overall (LOA) where LOA = length of hull excluding bowsprit, bumkin, self-steering gear or externally hung rudder. Small yachts will not be permitted to enter if their original design or construction has been deliberately lengthened to reach or exceed the lower limit of 25ft LOA.

10. ENGINES AND POWER

10.1 No means of propulsion may be employed other than the force of the wind, the man-power of the crew or both.

10.2 An internal combustion engine, which must be incapable of being able to propel the yacht, may be used to generate electricity. This engine may be the yacht's auxiliary engine, provided that the propeller has been removed, or the shaft or gear lever sealed before the start. Where this is impracticable a yacht's engine must not be used for generating electricity.

10.3 Seals will be inspected upon arrival in Newport and should a seal have been broken for any reason this is to be stated on the Declaration Form. The Committee will then decide whether a penalty is appropriate.

10.4 Electricity may be used to operate a self-steering gear, but all sail handling must be performed by the man-power of the crew alone.

11. RECOGNITION

11.1 A distinguishing number must at all times be displayed on the yacht's hull, deck and sails. Yachts may use either their existing sail number or the race number which will be allocated to each entry on acceptance. They may NOT display any other number. Numbers are to be a minimum 12in, or 1/40th of the yacht's overall length, whichever is the larger.

11.2 Where a yacht's normal sail number has less than three digits she will be required to use her race number on the sails and hull as means of identification.

11.3 Markings on yachts' sides and decks are to be painted. Adhesive tape will not be accepted.

12. INSPECTION

Although no stipulations (except as stated elsewhere in these Rules) will be made as to design, construction, rig or equipment of yachts, each yacht will be required to pass the inspections after she has arrived in Plymouth (Rule 6.9).

(a) Safety and Rule Inspection by one or more persons appointed by the Committee. This is to inspect the equipment as required by the Special Regulations which follow these Rules and also to examine any other part of the yacht's design, construction or equipment which they consider to bear directly on the safety of yacht or crew.

(b) Inspection of Condition and Seaworthiness. Any yacht whose condition or seaworthiness appears doubtful will be further inspected by a team of not less than three experienced yachtsmen and one or more yacht surveyors.

(c) Size Limit Inspection to establish the class as laid down in Rule 9 and the lower and upper size limits. Where a yacht appears to be close to one of the upper size limits, or to the lower size limit, she will be measured by a measurer appointed by the RWYC. His decision will be final and there can be no appeal.

13. ACCEPTANCE CERTIFICATE

13.1 As soon as possible after passing the inspections the skipper will be issued with an Acceptance Certificate. Without this he will not be allowed to sail in the Race. It is the responsibility of the crew to obtain this Certificate from the Organizers before his yacht leaves Plymouth.

13.2 Yachts which do not receive an Acceptance Certificate will not be fitted with a System Argos Transmitter.

13.3 Yachts which have not qualified and been accepted for the race must not join the start of the race. Failure to observe this instruction may result in the skipper being refused entry into other races organized by the Royal Western Yacht Club.

14. YACHTS FAILING TO PASS INSPECTION

14.1 As soon as possible after each of the inspections the skipper will be notified in writing of any respect in which the yacht has failed to pass inspection. He will then be free either to remedy the defects and ask for a further inspection, or to accept disqualification.

14.2 There will be a briefing conference on Friday 1 June which all entrants and any reserve crews will be required to attend.

15. PENALTIES

The Committee reserves the right to impose a time penalty for any infringement of the letter or spirit of the Rules, and to apply this either in the form of a delayed start or a correction to the yacht's finishing time.

16. RADIO AND NAVIGATION AIDS

Radar and all radio aids to navigation are permitted.

17. SURVIVAL BEACON

A survival beacon operating on 121.5 and 243 MHz must be carried.

If the beacon is activated every effort must be made to switch it off when the skipper has been successfully rescued.

18. OUTSIDE ASSISTANCE

18.1 No physical contact, except for the passing of written messages, may be made with other ships or boats at sea, and no stores may be received from any ship or aircraft during the Race. They may, however, be asked for advice or information, and to report the yacht's position and condition.

18.2 During the Race a yacht may put in anywhere and anchor or moor for any purpose. She may be towed for a distance not exceeding two miles into, and for a distance not exceeding two miles out of any such harbour or anchorage, provided that the total result of such towage can be shown not to have advanced the yacht.

18.3 Yachts must sail the whole course independently and may not deliberately escort each other or arrange any other escort.

19. DECLARATION

Immediately after finishing each skipper will be required to sign a declaration that he has sailed the Race in accordance with all published Rules, or if any have been broken to give a full account of the circumstances, establishing to what, if any, extent the yacht's progress towards the finish was helped by the breach in question.

20. FINISHING

In order to qualify as a finisher a yacht must finish not later than 2359 Local Time on Saturday, 21 July 1984.

21. AUTHORITY

These Rules are published by the Royal Western

Yacht Club of England who reserves the right to amend or add to the Rules at any time up to the start of the Race, such amendments being immediately promulgated to all entrants who have been provisionally accepted. Additional instructions will in any case be issued by the Organizers to cover details of the starting and finishing arrangements.

22. PASSPORT AND VISA

22.1 Entrants will be required to furnish themselves with, and produce before the Race, valid documents for entry into the USA. A visa is necessary and entrants are advised to take advice on the documents necessary for entry into the UK before the Race.

22.2 Entrants should also provide for an adequate amount of dollar currency to meet their requirements after arrival in the USA.

Special Regulations Governing Navigational and Safety Equipment

OWNER'S RESPONSIBILITY

1. The safety of a yacht and her crew is the sole and inescapable responsibility of the Owner, or her Skipper who as the Owner's representative must do his best to ensure that the yacht is fully found, thoroughly seaworthy and manned by an experienced crew who is physically fit to face bad weather. He must be satisfied as to the soundness of hull, spars, rigging, sails and all gear. He must ensure that all safety equipment is properly maintained and stowed and that the crew knows where it is kept and how it is to be used.

2. Neither the establishment of these Special Regulations, nor the inspection of a yacht under these regulations in any way limits or reduces the complete and unlimited responsibility of the Owner or Owner's Representative.

3. It is the sole and exclusive responsibility of each Skipper to decide whether or not to start or continue to race.

INSPECTION

4. A yacht may be inspected at any time. If she does not comply with these Special Regulations her entry may be rejected, or she will be liable to disqualification or such other penalty as may be prescribed by the National Authority or the Race Organizers.

BASIC STANDARDS

5.1 All equipment shall:
(a) Function properly
(b) Be readily accessible

(c) Be of a type, size and capacity suitable and adequate for the intended use and size of the yacht.

*5.2 Yachts shall be either self-righting, or positively buoyant and fitted, in each hull having accommodation, with a watertight hatch of a minimum diameter of 450mm which can be opened from either the inside or the outside, and placed in such a way that it is not under water when the yacht is capsized.

5.3 Yachts shall be strongly built, watertight and capable of withstanding solid water, knockdowns and capsizes. They must be properly rigged, be fully seaworthy and must meet the standards set forth herein. (Properly rigged means (inter alia) that shrouds shall never be disconnected.)

5.4 Inboard engine installation shall be such that the engine, when running, can be securely covered, and that the exhaust and fuel supply systems are securely installed and adequately protected from the effects of heavy weather.

5.5 Yachts' equipment and fittings, particularly safety equipment, shall be securely fastened so as to remain in position should the yacht be capsized 180 degrees.

*5.6 All hulls in which there is no living acommodation shall have at least one watertight transverse bulkhead and the distance between two transverse watertight bulkheads shall not exceed 4 metres.

*5.7 All hulls longer than 15 metres and containing living accommodation shall have a watertight bulkhead within 15 per cent of the vessel's length of the bow and abaft the forward limit of the waterline.

STRUCTURAL FEATURES

6.1 The hull, including deck, coach roof and all other parts, shall form an integral, essentially watertight unit and any openings in it shall be capable of being immediately secured to maintain this integrity (see 5.1). For example, running rigging or control lines shall not compromise this watertight unit. Centreboard and daggerboard trunk shall not open into the interior of the hull.

*6.2 A watertight opening shall be fitted on every compartment where there is no living accommodation.

6.3 All hatches shall be permanently fitted so that they can be closed immediately and will remain firmly shut in a 180-degree capsize. The main companionway hatch shall be fitted with a strong positive securing arrangement which shall be operable from above and below.

6.4 Cockpits shall be structurally strong. They shall be watertight, so that no water can leak into the hull, from the cockpit by any opening placed at less than 40cm above the cockpit sole. They shall be self-draining, and shall drain at all angles of heel.

The cockpit sole shall be at least 2 per cent LOA above the waterline.

6.5   Storm coverings are to be provided for all windows more than two square feet in area unless they are made of a material at least as strong as the surrounding superstructure.

6.6   *Seacocks* or *valves* are to be fitted on all through-hull openings below the waterline except integral deck scuppers, shafts or log, speed indicators, depth finders and the like. However, a means of closing such openings, when necessary to do so, shall be provided.

6.7   *Ballast and Heavy Equipment.* Inside ballast in a yacht shall be securely fastened in position. All other heavy internal fittings (such as batteries, stoves, gas bottle, tanks, engines, outboard motors, etc.) and anchors and chains shall be securely fastened against a capsize.

LIFELINES, STANCHIONS AND PULPITS

7.1   One of the two following systems for personal safety shall be fitted:

(a) *MONOHULLS* and *MULTIHULLS*. Pulpits and lifelines fitted continuously all round the working deck with a minimum height of 60cm above the local deck, with an intermediate lifeline. These lifelines shall enclose all permanent stays. They shall be permanently supported at intervals of not more than 2.13 metres (7ft) by stanchions and pulpits which shall be through-bolted or welded.

When the cockpit opens aft to the sea, additional lifelines must be fitted so that no opening is greater in height than 56cm (22in).

OR

(b) *MULTIHULLS ONLY*. Pulpits as in (a) above and anchor points for the attachment of safety harnesses in such numbers and places that any point on deck may be reached with the harness attached.

In both cases, non-self-righting yachts shall also be equipped with safety harness anchorage points on and beneath the hull(s).

7.2   A toe rail of not less than 25mm shall be permanently fitted around the deck forward of the mast, except in way of fittings. Location to be not further inboard from the edge of the working deck than one-third of the local beam.

ACCOMMODATION

8.1   Toilet, securely installed, or fitted bucket.

8.2   Bunks securely installed.

8.3   Cooking stove, securely installed against a capsize with safe, accessible fuel shut-off control capable of being safely operated in a seaway.

8.4   At least three securely installed water tanks or properly secured containers so that drinkable water may be held in different tanks/containers.

GENERAL EQUIPMENT

9.1   One fire extinguisher, readily accessible and at least two in yachts with an engine or a heater, one of which must be not less than 1.36kg.

9.2   Bilge Pumps, at least two manually operated. Securely fitted to the yacht's structure, one operable above, the other below deck. Each pump shall be operable with all the cockpit seats, hatches and companionways shut.

9.3   Unless permanently fitted, each bilge pump handle shall be provided with a lanyard or catch or similar device to prevent accidental loss.

9.4   Yachts that are not self-righting shall have a portable manual bilge-pump with which any water-tight compartment can be dried, or any equivalent system.

9.5   Two buckets of stout construction each with at least 9 litres capacity. Each bucket to have a lanyard.

9.6   Anchors. Two anchors provided with an adequate combination of chain and warp.

9.7   Flashlights, one of which is suitable for signalling, water resistant, with spare batteries and bulbs.

9.8   First Aid kit and manual.

9.9   Radar reflector. If the radar reflector is octahedral it must have a minimum diagonal measurement of 42cm or, if not octahedral, must have an equivalent echoing area of not less than $10m^2$.

9.10   Shut-off valves on all fuel tanks.

NAVIGATION EQUIPMENT

10.1   Compass, marine type, properly installed and adjusted.

10.2   Spare compass.

10.3   Charts, light lists, pilotage equipment.

10.4   Sextant, nautical almanac, accurate time-piece.

10.5   Radio direction finder.

10.6   Lead line or echo sounder.

10.7   Log for measuring distance sailed.

10.8   Navigation lights, to be shown as required by the International Regulations for the Prevention of Collision at Sea, mounted so that they will not be masked by the sails or the heeling of the yacht.

EMERGENCY EQUIPMENT

11.1   Yachts must carry suitable storm canvas capable of taking the yacht to windward. Any storm or heavy-weather jib if designed for a seastay or luff-groove device shall have an alternative method of attachment to the stay or a wire luff.

11.2   No mast shall have less than two halyards each capable of hoisting a sail.

11.3   *Emergency steering equipment.*

All yachts shall carry an emergency tiller capable

of being fitted to the rudder stock. Crews must be aware of alternative methods of steering the yacht in the event of a total rudder failure in any sea condition. An inspector may require this method to be demonstrated.

11.4　Tools and spare parts including adequate means to disconnect or sever the standing rigging from the hull in case of need.

11.5　Yacht's name on the liferaft and miscellaneous buoyant equipment such as life jackets, oars, cushions, etc.

11.6　Yachts shall carry an emergency position indicator beacon transmitting on 121.5 and 143 MHz.

11.7　Radio receiver capable of receiving weather bulletins.

SAFETY EQUIPMENT

12.1　Life jacket.

12.2　Whistle attached to life jacket.

12.3　Safety belt (Harness type). Yachts may be required to demonstrate that the crew can be adequately attached to strong points on the yacht.

12.4　Liferaft meeting the following requirements:

Must be carried on deck (not under dinghy) or in a special stowage opening immediately to the deck containing liferaft only.

Must be designed specifically for saving life at sea.

Must have at least two separate buoyancy compartments, each of which must be automatically inflatable: each raft must be capable of carrying its rated capacity with one compartment deflated.

Must have a canopy to cover the occupants.

Must have been inspected, tested and approved within 10 months by the manufacturer or other competent authority.

Must have the following equipment appropriately secured to each raft:

Sea anchor or drogue

1 bellows, pump or other means for maintaining inflation of air chambers

1 signalling light

3 hand flares

1 baler

1 repair kit

2 paddles

1 knife.

12.5　Provision for water and rations to accompany raft.

12.6　Distress signals to be stowed in a waterproof container

12 Red parachute flares

4 Red hand flares

4 White hand flares

2 Orange smoke day signals

12.7　Heaving line (50ft (16m) minimum length) readily accessible to cockpit.

* Regulations marked thus to apply to all yachts launched after 1 October 1982.

ROYAL WESTERN/OBSERVER SINGLEHANDED TRANSATLANTIC RACE, 1984

Form of Entry

To: The Secretary, Royal Western Yacht Club of England, 9 Grand Parade, Plymouth, Devon PL1 3DG

Name of Yacht..................................Rig..............................
Nationality of skipper............Class/Design of Yacht............
Type:　Single　Hull*/Trimaran*/Catamaran*/Proa*　Hull Colour ....
LOA.............LWL.............Beam.............Draught ....
Owner ....

Skipper's Name ....
Address ....
.... Tel. No...............

I..DECLARE that I am over the age of 21 years and that I wish to enter the above yacht for the Singlehanded Transatlantic Race and in the event of my entry being accepted I agree (a) that the sponsors and organizers of the Race shall have no liability either to me or my estate for any accident or loss arising consequent upon my entry and participation in the said Race and (b) to indemnify the sponsors and organizers of the Race in respect of any liability or loss whatsoever and howsoever arising consequent upon my entry and participation in the said Race whether such liability or loss shall be incurred in respect of myself, the yacht, third parties, another entrant in the Race or in any other respect.

I declare that the yacht's name is*/is not* related to sponsorship of the yacht or her skipper.

I accept the jurisdiction of the Organizers on all matters to do with the eligibility and disqualification.

I accept the jurisdiction of the Organizers on all matters to do with trophies and awards.

I agree to assist the Organizers by doing all I can to send back position and condition reports during the course of the Race.

I enclose herewith the sum of £　　being my entrance fee*/I have arranged for the sum of £　　to be transferred to a/c No. 05033640 at the National Westminster Bank Ltd., St. Andrews Cross, Plymouth*

* Delete as necessary

Signed ....
In the presence of (witness)...
Address of Witness...
....
Occupation of Witness..
Date..
(Particulars of Sailing Experience to be entered on the back of this form.)

SINGLE HANDED TRANS ATLANTIC RACE

1960-1984

ENTRIES

The information on the following pages is based on entry lists published by the Royal Western Yacht Club. Yachts that finished are listed according to their final position in the race. Where the name of a yacht has changed since the lists were published, the name under which she sailed has been given.

Abbreviations

C catamaran	Ret retired
M monohull	NS non-starter
P proa	Out out of time
T trimaran	Dis disqualified

1960

Yacht	Time Days: Hours	Crew	Nationality	Type
Gipsy Moth III (1)	40	Francis Chichester	British	M
Jester (2)	48	Blondie Hasler	British	M
Cardinal Vertue (3)	56	David Lewis	British	M
Eira (4)	63	Val Howells	British	M
Cap Horn (5)	74	Jean Lacombe	French	M

1964

Yacht	Time Days: Hours	Crew	Nationality	Type
Pen Duick II (1)	27:03	Eric Tabarly	French	M
Gipsy Moth III (2)	29:23	Francis Chichester	British	M
Akka (3)	32:18	Val Howells	British	M
Lively Lady (4)	36:17	Alec Rose	British	M
Jester (5)	37:22	Blondie Hasler	British	M
Stardrift (6)	38:03	Bill Howell	Australian	M
Rehu Moana (7)	38:12	David Lewis	British	C
Ilala (8)	46:06	Mike Ellison	British	M
Golif (9)	46:07	Jean Lacombe	French	M
Vanda Caelea (10)	49:18	Bob Bunker	British	M
Misty Miller (11)	53:00	Mike Butterfield	British	C
Ericht 2 (12)	60:11	Geoffrey Chaffey	British	M
Folatre (13)	61:14	Derek Kelsall	British	T
Marco Polo (14)	63:13	Axel Pederson	Danish	M
Tammy Norie	Ret	Robin McCurdy	British	M

1968

Yacht	Time Days: Hours	Crew	Nationality	Type
Sir Thomas Lipton (1)	25:20	Geoffrey Williams	British	M
Voortrekker (2)	26:13	Bruce Dalling	South African	M
Cheers (3)	27:00	Tom Follett	U.S.	P
Spirit of Cutty Sark (4)	29:10	Leslie Williams	British	M
Golden Cockerel (5)	31:16	Bill Howell	Australian	C
Opus (6)	34:08	Brian Cooke	British	M
Gancia Girl (7)	34:13	Martin Minter-Kemp	British	T
Myth of Malham (8)	36:01	N. T. J. Bevan	British	M
Maxine (9)	37:13	B. de Castelbajac	French	M
Maguelonne (10)	38:09	Jean-Yves Terlain	French	M
Dogwatch (11)	38:12	N. S. A. Burgess	British	M
Sylvia II (12)	40:00	André Foezon	French	M
Fione (13)	40:14	Lt. B. Enbom	Swedish	M
Mex (14)	41:10	Claus Hehner	German	M
Rob Roy (15)	42:03	Rev. S. W. Pakenham	British	M

1968

Yacht	Time Days:Hours	Crew	Nationality	Type
Startled Faun (**16**)	45:10	Colin Forbes	British	T
Amistad (**17**)	47:18	B. Rodriguez	U.S.	T
Goodwin II (**18**-Dis)		Ake Matteson	Swedish	M
Jester (**19**)	57:10	Michael Richey	British	M
Pen Duick	Ret	Eric Tabarly	French	T
Hera	NS	A. Welsh	Norwegian	M
Coila	Ret	Eric Williams	British	T
Kytra II	NS	G. U. Goodbody	British	M
Axel Heyst III	NS	W. L. Higgins	U.S.	M
San Giorgio	Ret	Alex Carozzo	Italian	C
Atlantis III	Ret	David Pyle	British	M
Wileca	Ret	W. Wallin	Swedish	M
Genesis	NS	L. E. Osborne	British	T
Tamoure	Ret	B. Waquet	French	T
Koala III	Ret	Edith Baumann	German	T
Kathena	NS	W. Erdmann	German	M
Zeevalk	Ret	R. G. N. Wingate	British	M
White Ghost	Ret	M. J. Pulsford	British	M
Aye-Aye	Ret	Egon Heinemann	German	M
Guntur III	Ret	Guy Piazzini	Swiss	M
Ocean Highlander	Ret	A. Munro	British	C
La Delirante	Ret	L. Paillard	French	M
Neptune	NS	Alain Gliksman	French	M
Yaksha	NS	Joan de Kat	French	T
Aigrette	NS	Olivier de Kersauson	French	T
Ambrima	Ret	Marc Cuiklinski	French	M
Vif Argent	NS	H. Garreta	French	M

1972

Yacht	Time Days:Hours	Crew	Nationality	Type
Pen Duick IV (**1**)	20:13	Alain Colas	French	T
Vendredi Treize (**2**)	21:05	Jean-Yves Terlain	French	M
Cap 33 (**3**)	24:05	Jean-Marie Vidal	French	T
British Steel (**4**)	24:19	Brian Cooke	British	M
Three Cheers (**5**)	27:11	Tom Follett	U.S.	T
Architeuthis (**6**)	28:11	Gérard Pesty	French	T
Strongbow (**7**)	28:12	Martin Minter-Kemp	British	M
Toucan (**8**)	28:12:54	Alain Gliksman	French	M
Sagittario (**9**)	28:23	Franco Faggioni	Italian	M
Whisper (**10**)	29:11	James Ferris	U.S.	M
Isles du Frioul (**11**)	30:02	Marc Linski	French	M
Polonez (**12**)	30:16	Krzysztof Baranowski	Polish	M
Binkie II (**13**)	31:18	Mike McMullen	British	M
Aloa VII (**14**)	32:22	Marie-Claude Fauroux	French	M

1972 Yacht	Time Days:Hours	Crew	Nationality	Type
Flying Angel (15)	33:09	Lt.Col. P. Brazier	British	M
White Rocket (16)	34:13	Joël Charpentier	French	M
Aloa I (17)	34:17	Yves Olivaux	French	M
Cambronne (18)	35:10	Guy Piazzini	French	M
Concorde (19)	36:01	Pierre Chassin	French	M
Gazelle (20)	36:02	Bruce Webb	British	M
La Bamba of Mersea (21)	36:04	John Holtom	British	M
Blue Smoke (22)	36:21	Lt. Guy Hornett, R.N.	British	M
White Dolphin (23)	38:07	Wolf-Dietrich Kirchner	German	M
Ron Glas (24)	38:09	Jock McLeod	British	M
Shamaal (25)	38:10	Richard Clifford	British	M
Blue Gipsy (26)	39:08	R. Lancy Burn	U.S.	M
Trumpeter (27)	39:13	Phil Weld	U.S.	T
Mex (28)	40:08	Claus Hehner	German	M
Surprise (29)	41:04	Ambrogio Fogar	Italian	M
Mary Kate of Arun (30)	41:17	Capt. P. C. S. Chilton, R.N.	British	M
Francette (31)	43:09	Lt.Cdr. (S.C.C.) Eric Sumner, R.N.R.	British	M
Miranda (32)	45:10	Zbigniew Puchalski	Polish	M
Tinie (33)	46:15	Heiko Krieger	German	M
Scuffler III (34)	49:02	Jerry Cartwright	U.S.	M
Lauric (35)	51:14	Christopher Elliott	British	M
Summersong (36)	51:23	Andrew Spedding	British	M
Willing Griffin (37)	52:11	David Blagden	British	M
Komodor (38)	57:03	Teresa Remiszewska	Polish	M
Jester (39)	58:08	Michael Richey	British	M
P.S. (40)	59:06	Anne Michailof	French	M
Leen Valley Venturer	NS	John M. Beswick	British	T
Bristol Fashion	Ret	Sqdn. Ldr. A. E. M. Barton	British	M
Namar IV	Ret	Edoardo Guzzetti	Italian	M
Chica Boba	Ret	Carlo Mascheroni	Italian	M
Tuloa	Ret	H. G. Mitchell	British	M
Tahiti Bill	Ret	Bill Howell	Australian	C
Mersea Pearl	Ret	Bob Miller	British	M
Niké	Out	Richard Konkolski	Czech.	M
Second Life	Ret	Gerard Dijkstra	Dutch	M
Myth of Malham	NS	Jean-Pierre Levaire	French	M
Olva II	Ret	Oscar E. Debra	Belgian	M
Casper	Out	Martin Wills	British	M
White Lady	NS	Hubert Bargholtz	Swedish	M
Gipsy Moth V	Ret	Francis Chichester	British	M
Lady of Fleet	Ret	Murray Sayle	Australian	C
Golden Vanity	Out	Peter Crowther	British	M
Justa Listang	Ret	Bob Salmon	British	M
Onyx	Ret	Eugene Riguidel	French	M
Tang'O	NS	Gérard Curvelier	French	M

1976

Classes were introduced in 1976: Pen Duick (P) for yachts over 65ft long; Gipsy Moth (GM), 38ft to 65ft; Jester (J), up to 38ft.

Yacht	Time Days:Hours	Crew	Nationality	Class	Type
Pen Duick VI (1)	23:20	Eric Tabarly	French	P	M
Club Méditerranée (2)	24:03	Alain Colas	French	P	M
The Third Turtle (3)	24:20	Mike Birch	Canadian	J	T
Spaniel (4)	24:23	Kazimierz Jaworski	Polish	J	M
Cap 33 (5)	26:08	Tom Grossman	U.S.	P	T
Petrouchka (6)	27:00	Jean Claude Parisis	French	GM	M
F.T. (7)	27:07	David Palmer	British	J	T
Friends (8)	27:10	Walter Greene	U.S.	J	T
Arauna IV (9)	27:15	Jacques Timsit	French	GM	M
Objectif Sud 3 (10)	28:09	Alain Gabbay	French	J	M
Moonshine (11)	28:12	Francis Stokes	U.S.	GM	M
Venilia (12)	29:00	Carlo Bianchi	Italian	GM	M
Robertson's Golly (13)	29:01	Clare Francis	British	J	M
Tyfoon V (14)	29:21	Gustav Versluys	Belgian	J	M
Quest (15)	30:07	John de Trafford	British	GM	T
Pawn of Nieuwpoort (16)	30:15	Yves Anrys	Belgian	J	M
Nova (17)	30:15	Eugene Riguidel	French	J	T
Ackel France (18)	31:03	Gilles Vaton	French	J	M
Lorca (19)	31:14	Daniel Pierre	French	J	M
Sirtec (20)	31:23	Patrice Dumas	French	GM	M
Old Moore's Almanac (21)	32:02	Guy Hornett	British	GM	T
Tahiti Bill (22)	32:05	Bill Howell	Australian	GM	C
Wild Rival (23)	32:13	Geoff Hales	British	J	M
Petit Breton (24)	32:19	Bernard Pallard	French	J	M
Dadztoy II (25)	32:20	Folkmar Graf	German	J	M
Carina (26)	33:01	Ernesto Raab	Italian	GM	M
Adhara (27)	33:02	Rome Ryott	British	J	M
Pierre (28)	33:03	Pierre Riboulet	French	J	M
Helene III (29)	33:08	Gerd Bucking	German	J	M
Shamaal II (30)	33:12	Richard Clifford	British	J	M
Wind Quest (31)	34:08	E. Everett-Smith	U.S.	GM	M
Pytheas (32)	34:10	Burg Veenemans	Dutch	J	M
Azulao (33)	35:03	Nicholas Clifton	British	J	T
Innovator of Mana (34)	35:12	John Mansell	New Zealander	J	M
Fromstock Filius (35)	35:16	Philip Howells	British	J	M
Freemerle (36)	35:22	D. K. Clark	British	J	M
Kor Karoli (37)	36:01	Georgi Georgiev	Bulgarian	J	M
Patriarche (38)	36:05	Yves Olivaux	French	J	M
Jabulisiwe (39)	36:08	Ian Radford	British	J	M
Swedlady (40)	36:11	Lars Wallgren	Swedish	J	M
Chica Boba (41)	37:06	Edoardo Austoni	Italian	GM	M
Eva (42)	37:08	Ida Castiglioni	Italian	J	M

1976

Yacht	Time Days:Hours	Crew	Nationality	Class	Type
Evaloa (**43**)	37:10	Elie Labourgade	French	J	M
Lilliam (**44**)	37:21	Klaus Schrodt	German	J	M
Ron Glas (**45**)	38:17	Jock McLeod	British	GM	M
Edith (**46**)	39:04	Rory Nugent	U.S.	J	T
Achilles Neuf (**47**)	39:06	Chris Butler	British	J	M
Crisan (**48**)	39:08	Juan Guiu	Spanish	GM	M
Niké (**49**)	39:10	Richard Konkolski	Czech.	J	M
English Rose IV (**50**)	39:11	James Young	British	J	M
Galway Blazer (**51**)	39:12	Peter Crowther	British	GM	M
Catapha (**52**)	39:17	David White	U.S.	J	M
Tuloa (**53**)	41:11	H. G. Mitchell	British	J	M
Castanuela (**54**)	42:10	Enrique Vidal Paz	Spanish	J	M
Westward (**55**)	42:10	David Pyle	British	J	M
Miranda (**56**)	42:13	Zbigniew Puchalski	Polish	GM	M
Amitie (**57**)	42:17	Wolfgang Wanders	German	J	M
Hesperia (**58**)	42:21	Henk Jukkema	Dutch	J	M
Achille (**59**)	43:08	Max Bourgeois	French	J	M
Tikka III (**60**)	44:00	Corrado Di Majo	Italian	J	M
Lady Anne of St Donats (**61**)	44:03	David Sutcliffe	British	J	M
Caipirinha (**62**)	44:04	Angelo Preden	Italian	J	M
Golden Harp (**63**)	44:19	Stuart Woods	Irish	J	M
Casper (**64**)	44:21	Martin Wills	British	J	M
Lauric (**65**)	45:02	Richart Elliott	British	J	M
Janina (**66**)	45:03	Henry Pottle	British	J	M
Dragon (**67**)	45:12	Michel Bourgeois	French	GM	M
Airedale (**68**)	46:11	D. S. Cowper	British	J	M
Galadriel of Lothlorien (**69**)	48:03	Nigel Lang	British	J	M
Songeur (**70**)	49:05	Rodney Kendall	New Zealander	J	M
Bestevaer (**71**)	49:07	Gerard Dijkstra	Dutch	GM	M
Bylgia (**72**)	49:10	Eilco Kasemier	Dutch	GM	M
Prodigal (**73**)	49:19	Bob Lengyel	U.S.	J	M
Galloping Gael	Missing	Mike Flanagan	U.S.	J	M
Bollemaat IV	Ret	Kees Roemers	Dutch	GM	M
Tinie II	Ret	Heiko Krieger	German	J	M
Jade	Ret	R. J. Ogle	British	GM	M
True North	Out	Brian Start	Canadian	J	M
Kylie	Ret	Simon Hunter	British	J	M
Flying Angel	Ret	Jock Brazier	British	GM	M
Silke	Ret	Hans Joachim Schulte	German	J	M
Manureva	NS	Jean Francois Colas	French	P	T
Jester	Ret	Michael Richey	British	J	M
Unibrass Brython	Ret	Val Howells	British	J	M
Spirit of Surprise	Ret	Ambrogio Fogar	Italian	J	C
ITT Oceanic	Ret	Yvon Fauconnier	French	P	M
Aquarius	Ret	Andre De Jong	Dutch	J	M
Toria	Ret	Tony Bullimore	British	GM	T

1976 Yacht	Time Days:Hours	Crew	Nationality	Class	Type
Kriter III	Ret	Jean-Yves Terlain	French	P	C
Bluff	Out	Rod White	British	J	M
Ek Soeki	Ret	John Christian	British	J	M
Gauloises	Ret	Pierre Fehlmann	Swiss	GM	M
Acteia II	Ret	Christian le Merrer	French	J	M
Mex	NS	Claus Hehner	German	J	M
Namar 5	Ret	Edoardo Guzzetti	Italian	GM	M
Martina	NS	Piero Nessi	Italian	J	M
Valitalia	Ret	Paolo Sciarretta	Italian	GM	M
Sexaginta Prista	NS	Rumen Peev	Bulgarian	GM	M
Bris	NS	Sven Lundin	Swedish	J	M
Karate	Ret	Pierre-Yves Charbonnier	French	J	M
Meinwen	Out	Peter Evans	British	J	M
Whisper	NS	James Ferris	U.S.	GM	M
Spirit of America	Ret	Michael Kane	U.S.	P	T
Gazelle	NS	Bruce Webb	British	GM	M
Great Britain III	NS	Chay Blyth	British	P	T
Bigouden Brise	Out	Jean Ropert	French	J	M
Lady Garuda	NS	Wolfgang Quix	German	J	M
Tumult	Ret	Chris Smith	British	J	M
McArthur	Ret	Hywell Price	British	J	M
Three Cheers	Missing	Mike McMullen	British	GM	T
Pen-Ar-Bed	Ret	Gerard Frigout	French	GM	M
CS & RB II-Busnelli	Ret	Doi Malingri di Bagnolo	Italian	GM	M
Objectif Sud 1	Ret	Marc Linski	French	J	M
Objectif Sud 2	NS	Christian Hollier	French	J	M
Jan	NS	Hamilton Ferris	U.S.	J	T
Demon Demo	Ret	Angus Primrose	British	J	M
Altergo	Ret	C. S. W. Ward	British	GM	M
5100	Ret	Dominique Berthier	French	GM	M
Silmaril	Ret	Patrick O'Donovan	Eire	J	T
One Hand Clapping	NS	Anthony Lush	U.S.	J	M
White Dolphin	NS	Wolf-Dietrich Kirchner	German	J	M
Croda Way	Ret	Mike Best	British	GM	T
Kervilor	Ret	Guy Cornou	French	J	M
Keep Cap D'Agde	Ret	Jean Claud Montesinos	French	GM	M
Aleph	NS	Mario Pirri	Italian	GM	M
Panda 31	Ret	Paolo Mascheroni	Italian	J	M
Arctic Skua	Ret	Mike Richardson	British	J	M
Gillygaloo	Ret	Andrew Bray	British	J	M
Sleuth Hound	Ret	Colin Drummond	British	J	M
Ballyclaire	Out	Dr. F. Sloan	British	J	M
Wild Rocket	Ret	Joël Charpentier	French	P	M
Logo	Ret	Aline Marchand	French	J	M
Nyarlathotep	Ret	P. Szekely	French	GM	M
Ro	NS	Antonino Giammarce	Italian	GM	M

1976 Yacht	Time Days:Hours	Crew	Nationality	Class	Type
Ironiguy	Ret	Guy Brunet	French	J	M
Sharavoge	Ret	Johnathan Virden	British	J	M
Depollution	NS	Guy Bernardin	French	GM	M
Pronuptia	Ret	C. H. le Moing	French	GM	M
Grand Large	NS	Pierre English	French	P	T
Drakkar III	Ret	Alain Marcel	French	GM	M
Pallas	NS	Yann Nedellec	French	J	M
Vanessa	Ret	Oscar E. Debra	Belgian	GM	M

1980

There was a length restriction for the first time. The classes were:
Pen Duick (P), 44ft to 56ft; Gipsy Moth (GM), 32ft to 44ft; Jester (J), 25ft to 32ft.

Yacht	Time Days:Hours	Crew	Nationality	Class	Type
Moxie (1)	17:23	Phil Weld	U.S.	P	T
Three Legs of Man III (2)	18:06	Nick Keig	British	P	T
Jeans Foster (3)	18:06	Philip Steggall	U.S.	GM	T
Olympus Photo (4)	18:07	Mike Birch	Canadian	P	T
Chaussettes Olympia (5)	18:17	Walter Greene	U.S.	GM	T
Spaniel II (6)	19:13	Kazimierz Jaworski	Polish	P	M
Chica Boba II (7)	20:02	Edoardo Austoni	Italian	P	M
Brittany Ferries (8)	21:00	Daniel Gilard	French	GM	M
Nike II (9)	21:06	Richard Konkolski	Czech	GM	M
Kriter VII (10)	21:08	Tom Grossman	U.S.	P	T
Stadt Krefeld (11)	21:14	Wolfgang Wanders	German	GM	M
Tyfoon VI (12)	21:15	Gustav Versluys	Belgian	GM	M
Hydrofolie (13)	21:16	Alain Labbe	French	GM	T
Kriter VI (14)	21:20	Olivier de Kersauson	French	P	M
Guia IV Fila (15)	22:02	Pierre Sicouri	Italian	P	M
Boatfile (16)	22:22	Rob James	British	GM	T
France Loisirs (17)	23:10	Denis Gliksman	French	GM	M
Voortrekker (18)	23:12	Bertie Reed	South African	P	M
V.S.D. (19)	24:01	Eugene Riguidel	French	P	T
Haute-Nendaz (20)	24:03	Philippe Fournier	Swiss	GM	M
Open Space (21)	25:01	Jean Pierre Millet	French	P	M
Garuda (22)	25:08	Victor Sagi	Spanish	P	M
Mooneshine (23)	25:14	Francis Stokes	U.S.	GM	M
Kriter Lady (24)	25:19	Naomi James	British	P	M
Third Turtle (25)	25:20	William Homewood	U.S.	GM	T
Ambergris (26)	26:00	Robert Bocinsky	U.S.	GM	M
Les Menuires (27)	26:15	Jean Jacques Jaouen	French	GM	M
Spaniel (28)	26:19	Jerzy Rakowicz	Polish	GM	M
Le First (29)	26:22	Jerry Cartwright	U.S.	J	M
Free Newspapers (30)	28:00	John Chaundy	British	J	M
Edith (31)	28:04	William Doelger	U.S.	GM	T
Yoldia (32)	28:05	Uno Hylen	Swedish	GM	M
Wild Rival (33)	28:13	Desmond Hampton	British	GM	M

1980

Yacht	Time Days:Hours	Crew	Nationality	Class	Type
Atlantic Harp **(34)**	29:06	John Charnley	British	GM	M
Jabulisiwe **(35)**	30:14	Ian Radford	British	J	M
Basildon Moonshadow **(36)**	30:15	John Oswald	British	GM	M
Crumpy Nut **(37)**	30:16	Oscar E. Debra	Belgian	GM	M
Warrior Shamaal **(38)**	30:16	Richard Clifford	British	GM	M
Victoria **(39)**	30:18	Henk Jukkema	Dutch	J	M
Sadler Bluejacket **(40)**	30:19	Chris Smith	British	J	M
Achillea **(41)**	30:20	Chris Butler	British	J	M
Bollemaat IV **(42)**	30:21	Kees Roemers	Dutch	GM	M
Demon of Hamble **(43)**	30:23	Angus Primrose	British	GM	M
Parisien Liberé **(44)**	31:10	Roger Forkert	French/U.S.A.	GM	T
Ratso II **(45)**	31:11	Guy Bernardin	French	GM	M
Dream Weaver **(46)**	31:23	James H. Kyle	U.S.	J	M
Cat Marine **(47)**	32:02	Alain Veyron	French	J	T
Abacus **(48)**	32:07	D. K. Clark	British	GM	M
Mistral **(49)**	32:18	Thomas Gochberg	U.S.	GM	M
Egret **(50)**	33:05	Luis Tonizzo	U.S.	J	M
Tangra **(51)**	34:10	Nikolay Jambazov	Bulgarian	GM	M
Black Pearl **(52)**	35:11	Wytze van der Zee	Dutch	GM	M
Northwind **(53)**	36:06	José Ugarte	Spanish	GM	M
Tjisje **(54)**	36:22	Hank van de Weg	Dutch	J	M
Christian Saul II **(55)**	37:03	Paul Rodgers	British	GM	T
Jeantex **(56)**	38:03	Wolfgang Quix	German	J	M
Cecco **(57)**	38:08	Giampaolo Venturin	Italian	J	M
Crisan **(58)**	38:13	Juan Guiu	Spanish	GM	M
Seagull II **(59)**	38:17	J. R. Verwoerd	Dutch	GM	M
Olympus Sailing **(60)**	39:01	Bob Lush	Canadian	J	M
One Hand Clapping II **(61)**	39:06	Anthony Lush	U.S.	J	M
La Peligrosa **(62)**	39:16	Andre De Jong	Dutch	J	M
Prodigal **(63)**	40:06	Bob Lengyel	U.S.	J	M
Peggy **(64)**	40:20	Tom Ryan	U.S.	GM	T
Elbe **(65)**	41:10	Ernest Sonne	U.S.	GM	M
Crystal Catfish III **(66)**	41:13	John Hunt	U.S.	J	M
Miscin **(67)**	42:16	John Beharrell	British	GM	M
Mu Lat **(68)**	42:18	Beppe Panada	Italian	P	M
Mare **(69)**	42:23	Per Mustelin	Finnish	J	M
Novia **(70)**	44:10	William Wallace	U.S.	J	M
Casper **(71)**	46:13	Martin Wills	British	J	M
Pytheas II **(72)**	49:08	Burg Veenemans	Dutch	P	M
Paul Ricard (unofficial entry)	18:13	Marc Pajot	French	P	T
Miss Dubonnet	Ret	Florence Arthaud	French	P	M
Fifi	NS	Peter Evans	British	GM	C
Jomada	Ret	Simon Hunter	British	J	M
Silke	Ret	Hans Joachim Schulte	German	GM	M
Miranda	NS	Zbigniew Puchalski	Polish	GM	M

1980

Yacht	Time Days:Hours	Crew	Nationality	Class	Type
Asparuh	NS	Dimitar Genchev	Bulgarian	GM	M
Jester	Out	Michael Richey	British	J	M
Arrival	NS	Joan Connors	U.S.	J	M
Serta Perfectsleeper	Ret	Judy Lawson	U.S.	GM	M
Arauna IV	NS	Yves Olivaux	French	GM	M
Galway Blazer of Dart	NS	Peter Crowther	British	GM	M
Troll Fjord	NS	Warren Holby	U.S.	GM	M
Old Navy Lights	Out	Anthony Vassiliadis	Greek	GM	M
Gudrun V	NS	Joaquin Coello	Spanish	GM	M
Maurice Lidchi	Ret	Michel Horeau	French	P	T
Great Britain IV	NS	Chay Blyth	British	P	T
Randori II	NS	Jack Larkin	British	GM	M
Tuesday's Child	Ret	Warren Luhrs	U.S.	P	M
Livery Dole	Ret	Peter Phillips	British	GM	T
Sea Quest	Ret	Mac Smith	U.S.	GM	M
Godiva Chocolatier	NS	Rory Nugent	U.S.	J	P
Racynski II	Ret	Czeslaw Gogolkiewicz	Polish	P	M
Roundabout	Ret	Theo Cockerell	British	GM	M
Pawn of Nieuwpoort	NS	Yves Anrys	Belgian	J	M
Lady Dona	Ret	Peter Laag	Dutch	GM	M
Quest	NS	Ian Worley	British	P	T
Alcyone	NS	Maurice Bernadet	French	GM	M
Brittany Ferries II	Ret	Bernard Pallard	French	J	M
Mattia III	Ret	Antonio Chioatto	Italian	GM	T
Gauloises IV	Ret	Eric Loizeau	French	P	T
Diddikai	NS	William Maney	U.S.	GM	M
Salamandre	NS	Guy Delage	French	GM	M
Fleury Michon	Ret	Nicholas Clifton	British	GM	P
Charles Heidsieck	Ret	Jean Claude Parisis	French	P	

1984

There was a new classification: Class I, 45ft to 60ft; Class II, 40ft to 45ft; Class III, 35ft to 40ft; Class IV, 30ft to 35ft; Class V, 25ft to 30ft.

Yacht	Time Days:Hours	Crew	Nationality	Class	Type
Umupro Jardin V (1)	16:06	Yvon Fauconnier	French	I	T
Fleury Michon (2)	16:12:25	Philippe Poupon	French	I	T
Elf Aquitaine II (3)	16:12:48	Marc Pajot	French	I	C
Paul Ricard (4)	16:14	Eric Tabarly	French	I	T
Travacrest Seaway (5)	16:17:23	Peter Phillips	British	I	T
Nantes (6)	16:17:51	Daniel Gilard	French	I	T
Region Centre (7)	16:19	Olivier Moussy	French	II	T
L'Aiglon (8)	16:20	Bruno Peyron	French	I	C
Ker Cadelac (9)	16:21	Francois Boucher	French	I	T

1984

Yacht	Time Days:Hours	Crew	Nationality	Class	Type
Thursday's Child (10)	16:22	Warren Luhrs	U.S.	I	M
Kermarine (11)	17:04	Vincent Levy	French	I	T
Mainstay Voortrekker (12)	17:22:02	John Martin	South African	I	M
Lessive St Marc (13)	17:22:17	Denis Gliksman	French	I	T
Destination St Croix (14)	18:12	Jack Petith	U.S.	III	T
Côte Basque (15)	18:13:34	Didier Munduteguy	French	II	T
Idenek (16)	18:13:49	Yves le Cornec	French	II	T
Gespac (17)	19:07	Philippe Fournier	Swiss	III	T
Sebago (18)	19:10:38	Walter Greene	U.S.	II	C
Chica Boba III (19)	19:10:41	Edoardo Austoni	Italian	I	M
City of Birmingham (20)	19:22	Tony Bullimore	British	III	T
City of Slidell (21)	20:23	Luis Tonizzo	U.S.	IV	M
Carteret Savings (22)	21:01	Jack Boye	U.S.	I	M
British Airways II (23)	21:05	Bill Homewood	U.S.	IV	T
Cenet (24)	21:06	Patrice Carpentier	French	II	M
Region de Picardie (25)	21:08	Alain Petit-Etienne	French	I	C
Patricia of Finland (26)	21:13	Kai Granholm	Finnish	III	M
Biscuits Lu (27)	21:18	Guy Bernardin	French	II	M
Survival Tech Group (28)	22:02	Anthony Lush	U.S.	IV	M
Orion Iru (29)	22:15	José Ugarte	Spanish	II	M
Ntombifuti (30)	22:16	Ian Radford	British	III	M
Big Shot (31)	22:18	Jim Bates	U.S.	IV	M
Vingt sur Vannes (32)	23:13	Alain Veyron	French	IV	C
Ms Patty (33)	24:14	John Shaw	British	III	C
Alcatel (34)	24:13	Olivier Dardel	French	III	M
Royal Leerdam (35)	24:18	Wijtze van der Zee	Dutch	III	M
Douche Champion (36)	25:03	Bruno Fehrenbach	French	IV	M
Betelgeuse (37)	25:05	Simon van Hagen	Dutch	II	M
LDS Sailor (38)	25:09	Henk Jukkema	Dutch	IV	M
La Baleine (39)	25:15	Colin Laird	Tobagan	II	M
Lone Eagle (40)	26:06	Tom Donnelly	U.S.	III	M
Jemima Nicholas (41)	26:18	Alan Wynne Thomas	British	III	M
Abacus (42)	27:11:11	Jerry Freeman	British	II	M
Sherpa Bill (43)	27:11:50	Alan Perkes	British	III	M
Gladiator (44)	28:04	David White	U.S.	I	M
Gamble Gold (45)	29:15	Brian O'Donoghue	British	IV	M
Quailo (46)	29:23	Mac Smith	U.S.	II	M
Olle P2 (47)	30:04	Hans van Hest	Dutch	III	M
Summer Salt (48)	30:12	Spence Langford	U.S.	III	M
Swansea Bay (49)	30:14	Chris Butler	British	V	M
Timpani (50)	30:23	Michael Serge de Petrovsky	British	V	M
Phagawi (51)	31:07	David Ryan	U.S.	V	M
El Torero (52)	31:08	Albert Fournier	U.S.	V	M
Lands End (53)	31:23	Robert Scott	U.S.	III	M
Sea-Beryl (54)	32:14	Bertus Buys	Dutch	IV	M
Shamrock (55)	32:15	Jan van Donselaar	Dutch	V	M

1984 Yacht	Time Days:Hours	Crew	Nationality	Class	Type
Mitsubishi Electric **(56)**	32:20	Alan Armstrong	British	V	M
Free Bird **(57)**	35:04	John Howie	U.S.	IV	M
Moustache **(58)**	35:15	Lloyd Hircock	Canadian	V	M
Gladys **(59)**	39:06	Dick Huges	Dutch	IV	M
Nord **(60)**	40:16	Vassil Kurtev	Bulgarian	V	M
Johan Lloyde **(61)**	41:04	Tim Hubbard	U.S.	IV	M
Meg of Muglins **(62)**	41:16	Jack Coffey	Irish	IV	M
De Volharding **(63)**	41:20	Goos Terschegget	Dutch	II	M
Crystal Catfish III **(64)**	44:14	John Hunt	U.S.	IV	M
Biotherm II	Ret	Florence Arthaud	French	I	T
33 Export	Ret	Gilles Gahinet	French	I	C
Marches de France	Ret	Michel Horeau	French	I	T
Colt Cars GB	Ret	Jeff Houlgrave	British	I	T
Crédit Agricole	Ret	Philippe Jeantot	French	I	C
Fury	Ret	Hugh McCoy	U.S.	I	C
Jet Services	Ret	Patrick Morvan	French	I	C
Lada Poch	Ret	Loick Peyron	French	I	C
Aliance Kaypro	Ret	Monique Brand	French	II	M
Roger & Gallet	Ret	Eric Loizeau	French	II	T
Tyfoon VI	Ret	Gustav Versluys	Belgian	II	M
Marsden	Ret	Frank Wood	British	II	T
Batchelor's Sweet Pea	Ret	June Clarke	British	III	T
Dancing Dolphin	Ret	Bob Menzies	British	III	M
Loiwing	Ret	Rachael Hayward	British	IV	M
La Peligrosa	Ret	Andre De Jong	Dutch	IV	M
Prodigal	Ret	Bob Lengyel	U.S.	IV	M
Double Brown	Ret	John Mansell	New Zealander	IV	C
Karpetz	Ret	Karl Peterzen	Swedish	IV	M
Jeremi V	Ret	Jean Jacque Vuylsteker	French	IV	M
Go Kart	Ret	David Duncombe	British	V	M
Quest for Charity	Ret	Geoff Hales	British	V	C
Refugee	NS (ill)	Douglas Parker	U.S.	V	M
Jester	Out	Michael Richey	British	V	M
Race Against Poverty	Ret	Chris Smith	British	V	M
Rizla +	Ret	Thomas Veyron	French	V	T
Tjisje	Ret	Hank van de Weg	Dutch	V	M
Novia	Ret	William Wallace	U.S.	V	M

BIBLIOGRAPHY

J.R.L. Anderson, *The Greatest Race in the World*, Hodder & Stoughton, London, 1964
Humphrey Barton, *Atlantic Adventures*, Adlard Coles Ltd., London, 1950
David Blagden, *Very Willing Griffin*, Peter Davies, London, 1973
Chay Blyth, *The Impossible Voyage*, Hodder & Stoughton, London, 1971
Alain Bombard, *Bombard's Voyage*, Methuen & Co., London, 1959
Vito Dumas, *Alone Through the Roaring Forties*, Adlard Coles Ltd., Southampton, 1960
T. Follett, D. Newick & J. Morris, *Project Cheers*, Adlard Coles Ltd., London, 1969
Daniel Gilles, *Alone*, Angus & Robertson, 1977
John Groser, *Atlantic Venture*, Ward Lock, London, 1968
Val Howells, *Sailing into Solitude*, Temple Press Books, London, 1966
Robin Knox-Johnston, *A World of my Own*, Cassell, London, 1969
Frank Page, *Alone Against the Atlantic*, Observer Ltd., 1980
Frank Page, *Solo to America*, Adlard Coles Ltd., London, 1972
Stephen Pakenham, *Separate Horizons*, Nautical Pub. Co.
Sir Alec Rose, *My Lively Lady*, Nautical Pub. Co., London, 1968
Eric Tabarly, *Pen Duick*, Adlard Coles Ltd., London, 1971
Nigel Tetley, *Trimaran Solo*, Nautical Pub. Co.
Philip S. Weld, *Moxie*, The Bodley Head, London, 1982
Geoffrey Williams, *Sir Thomas Lipton Wins*, Peter Davies, London, 1969

INDEX

Acknowledgements
We would like to thank all the people and organizations who provided illustrations for this book, including: Steve Benbow-Colorific 29b; Alistair Black 63t, 66, 67, 78, 79, 98, 99, 102, 106, 107, 109, 130, 131, 133t; Henri Bureau-Sygma 30, 83; James Clevett 56, 57; Jonathan Eastland 18b, 19, 59, 62, 63b, 85, 90, 91, 103, 176; Richard Farley 81; Bob Fisher 29t, 159r; Trevor Grove 133b; J. Guichard-Sygma 9 (Fauconnier), 12, 25, 142, 154, 156, 160t, 162, 163, 164, 170, 171; John Hillelson Agency 146bl, 146tcl, 166, 167, 168, 169; John Hodder 94, 126, 132; Image Bank 6, 7; Colin Jarman 17, 20, 21, 28t, 64 (Eyeline Features); J. Languevin-Sygma 146tl, 146tcr, 146tr, 146br; David Lawrence 38, 121; Barry Lewis 34; Eamonn McCabe 10, 11, 16, 18tl, 18r, 23, 28b, 31, 32, 58, 96, 116, 117, 136b, 140, 144, 145, 153, 155, 159t, 159l, 160b, 178, 179 (Phillips); Tony McGrath 56, 57; James Mortimer 148, 149, 150; The Observer 40, 46, 48, 49, 56, 57, 66, 67, 68, 80, 84, 88, 92, 93, 95, 105, 110, 111, 112, 119, 120b, 124b, 125t, 177, 181; RAF, St Mawgan, Crown copyright reserved, 52, 53; Mingam Rannou/Frank Spooner 65; Trevor Ridley 128, 137; Patrick Roach 26, 60, 174; Nick Rogers 14, 22, 24, 114, 138; Royal Western Yacht Club 36, 42, 43, 45, 129; Chris Smith 9 (Colas, Tabarly, Williams), 70, 179 (Richey), 184; James Stedman 172; Keith Taylor-Sail 87, 113, 120t, 122, 123, 124t, 125b, 134, 136t; Times Newspapers 73, 74, 75; Patrick Ward 9 (Chichester), 179 (Chichester).

Our thanks, too, to Sail magazine for permission to reproduce the articles by Phil Weld, Judy Lawson, Alain Colas and Jim Brown; and to Times Newspapers Limited for permission to reproduce articles by Murray Sayle, published in The Sunday Times on July 2 1972 and July 10 1972. The article by Alistair Cooke was first published in The Guardian, copyright © Alistair Cooke.